LONELINESS
– How to overcome it –

by Val Marriott and Terry Timblick

© 1988 Val Marriott and Terry Timblick

Published by Age Concern England
Bernard Sunley House
60 Pitcairn Road
Mitcham
Surrey CR4 3LL

Editor Lee Bennett
Design Eugenie Dodd
Production Joyce O'Shaughnessy
Typeset from disc by Parchment
(Oxford) Ltd
Printed by Ebenezer Baylis & Son Ltd
The Trinity Press, Worcester

ISBN 0 86242 077 6

Contents

Introduction

A collecting tin is rattled in the public's face for virtually every major disease and social adversity. Cancer and heart research, ill-treated children, lifeboatmen, the homeless. These are a few of the many, all deserving, causes that people are regularly asked to support by donation. But when did you last see a flag day for the lonely? Yet they far outnumber the total number embraced by other 'good causes'; and all of us, regardless of age, class, income and geographical location are potential victims of loneliness.

The word 'loneliness' is a vague term, but every sufferer knows only too well its spoiling, limiting, sapping effect. For many, feelings of loneliness and isolation are more than occasional shadows across their lives – they inflict intense futility or apparently incurable despair.

In this book we suggest two approaches to help you deal with loneliness – being positive and being creative. We also pinpoint opportunities for voluntary service and list some of the many self-help organisations. There may well be other groups in your area, their addresses are usually available at your local library, town hall or Citizen's Advice Bureau.

About the Authors

Val Marriott is a journalist and 'agony aunt'. The enormous volume of letters she receives every week on the subject of loneliness inspired her to collaborate with editor Terry Timblick, who has been involved with the agony column since it first began, to offer some guidelines on how to cope with, and hopefully conquer, the worst effects of being lonely and in despair. Val Marriott is married, with three children and four grandchildren. Her widowed mother lives with her in what is, often, a four-generation household.

What is Loneliness?

An interview with a psychologist

Psychologist Peter Honey specialises in helping people, at work and in their personal lives, to make better relationships with those about them. He is also the author of several books dealing with loneliness, and discusses the subject with Val Marriott in the interview below:

Q. **How do you define the problem?**
A. There are two kinds of loneliness: external which is caused by a situation, and internal which is brought about by thoughts, beliefs and attitudes that can isolate a person.

Being on a desert island would be an example of external loneliness, but the effect of being alone in a hostile world can be created, say, following a bereavement or the break-up of a relationship. People who suffer the most intense loneliness at such a time are those who are, to a great extent, dependent on others for the way they feel. True loneliness is created by both internal and external causes. In most people's minds this is something to be ashamed of, because an admission of being lonely is considered to be an admission of failure.

There are a lot of people who are not terribly happy with their own company and rely on others to make life interesting. This makes them vulnerable to both external and internal loneliness because they are not equipped to deal with a situation on their own.

External loneliness usually only lasts for a limited time. Grief after bereavement or the loneliness produced by an unhappy environment should not persist indefinitely unless the person involved is internally lonely as well. Everyone is prone to moments of external loneliness – that feeling of 'What am I doing here?' – when they want to run away from somebody or something, when they wish desperately that they were somewhere else. No one can prevent this feeling of panic, but they can recognise and, to some extent, control it.

Q. **What practical steps can people take to relieve their isolation?**

A. In a moment of external loneliness, I have said to myself 'For whatever reason, I'm stuck with this situation for a while. But it is still part of my life – time I'll never have again. Is it sensible to waste it in futile anger or anxiety?' The obvious answer is to take the initiative and try to change the situation for the better, for there is always something, however small, that can be done.

You also have to accept that on some days you will feel extra-vulnerable – unable to make any positive effort – but it does not mean that tomorrow you will *still* feel apathetic. It is far easier to do something practical about external rather than internal loneliness. You can improve your environment in many ways. But it is not addressing the deeper problem.

On your worst days you do not feel physically capable of re-arranging a room, going outside to talk to someone, or any of the things you are told you should do to relieve loneliness. This may be because your energy is directed towards feeling miserable instead of being used creatively.

Q. **How do you gain momentum when you're down?**
A. 'Getting up steam' – is very hard when you feel depressed and need all your concentration just to 'tick over'. Making an effort implies that you should rouse yourself, take responsibility, fight your way back into society. To attempt too much is to invite failure. You should take tiny steps forward, and gradually build upon your progress.

Lonely people often want a miracle to happen because it would be so much easier than the alternative – getting results bit by bit by making a sustained effort. This is where they may see a new relationship as the answer: to jump – on the rebound, after bereavement or divorce – into a new liaison which they dream will be a replica of what is past and over. This course of action rarely works, because the person involved is not yet at a stage to cope with the demands of such a relationship.

Q. **How can people come to terms with loneliness?**
A. Shy, introverted people may consider they are going to stay that way for life. But this is not so – everyone can modify their behaviour if they really want to, adding to their repertoire by small yet significant alterations. It is a 'cop out' to convince yourself that there is nothing you can do – that your situation is hopeless.

You may think everyone is luckier than you, and ask resentfully why you should be singled out – it just does not seem fair. Most people operate on an assumption that life is *supposed* to be fair! Whenever it is not, which is frequently, they become very upset because the world is doing them

wrong. Or perhaps they believe in a 'tit-for-tat' premise –
'If I try to be good and kind to everyone, I'm stacking up
points for my ultimate good'. Others may have a version of
God as the person who is responsible for what happens to
them, absolving themselves and making God the scapegoat.

They may also rationalise the circumstances and say 'God is
testing me' – whether the situation is a family bereavement
or a world famine, they class it as a test. Neither of these
approaches represents a healthy faith in a God who would
intervene in such a way. The fact is that no-one is born with
a copper-bottomed guarantee that life is going to be fair.

Loneliness can make a person too analytical and self-centred.
You think of yourself first, and of others only when their
actions and words relate to you. Everyone is either getting
on better than you, or doing the dirty on you. How much
better to try to stop thinking about yourself and put the
equivalent amount of energy into thinking about others.
Some of your feelings of isolation might then dissipate.
Loneliness is negative, and to translate negative impulses into
positive thought and action is to overcome them.

Q. How can you test whether you are giving out lonely vibes?

A. Tell-tale signs of loneliness in yourself and others would
include non-verbal behaviour and wearing a sad defeated
look. Lonely people may also dress in drab colours, thinking
'If I look bright people might notice me,' or 'Why should I
look cheerful when I don't feel cheerful?' Perhaps the words
of an American philosopher sum this up: 'Most people smile
when they are happy. I smile in order to feel happy'. But
no-one must, in any way, minimise the effort involved in
following such a course!

Loneliness can be off-putting to others in two aspects. Lonely people fail to 'meet you half way', are withdrawn and seem to be their own worst enemies. Or they can be 'all over you' – subjecting you to a verbal outpouring, a direct denial of the art of conversation, which is talking *with*, not *at*, people. It involves listening, asking questions, being truly interested in what others say. Lonely people ask fewer questions on average than others do, and even if they do ask questions, they do not always pay attention to the answers.

Loneliness is no respecter of persons. It attacks young and old, rich and poor alike. Modern circumstances contribute towards it environmentally, each family unit living within its own little 'box' and rarely communicating with its neighbours. City living (in spite of there being millions of other people around) is in many ways lonelier than rural living, where a small community sticks together for support, entertainment, perhaps even survival. Wherever you live, ageing also brings added resentment – you are growing older, losing your powers, feeling more alienated from young people as the years pass, yet somehow also at odds with your own age group.

Q. How do you begin to conquer loneliness?

A. Various reasons and conditions contribute to loneliness. The better you learn to face and understand them, the more likely you are to find the most effective means of conquering them. For instance, think how you would answer these questions:.

• How often do you feel lonely? Do certain times of the day, situations, etc. trigger it off?

• When do you feel less lonely – times when the feeling is not so oppressive?

• When you are with other people, how often do you initiate conversation or ask questions?

• How often do you talk about yourself? Do you really ask other people about themselves and afterwards, can you remember what they said?

• When was the last time you tried to do something positive to alter or improve your situation and/or feelings?

• When that attempt failed, did you decide it was hopeless and pointless to try again?

• Are you guilty of off-putting remarks to other people? When was the last time you said to somebody, 'How nice to see you'. How do you greet people?

Q. How can you stop feeling isolated?

A. Here are some positive suggestions:

• Keep track of lonely times during the past week, and decide which were the worst, and if possible, why. Try to recall what triggered off bad patches, and what you were able to do to feel that little bit better – perhaps when you were with other people, or achieved something through your own efforts. Think how you could work to increase the 'good' times.

• Try to equip yourself with various conversational 'levers' by reading newspapers, listening to the radio and watching the news on television (see also the further suggestions on pages 30-32). Make yourself really concentrate don't just listen to the sounds and look at the images.

• Think of past conversations – did you seize the opportunity to talk about your predicament and circumstances without realising that everyone else also has problems, worries and stress? Are you guilty of 'shutting off' when the conversation turns to others' views and worries rather than your own? Take every opportunity to listen more.

• Think of every day as an opportunity to take a step forward. True, you may often be knocked back a few paces, but it should not prevent the general forward progress, a little at a time. Don't give up – persistence is an ally, and you are the one who will ultimately benefit from your efforts.

• Although certain remarks you make may not imply criticism, put yourself in the position of someone who has come to visit you. To be greeted with 'Hello stranger' makes them wish they had not bothered to come at all, if what they get is a put-down. 'I thought it was about time you came' or 'What do you want?' are equally dismissive opening comments. On the other hand, a welcome, and a warm greeting make others glad they called to see you and likely to return.

Putting Your Problems Into Words

Val Marriott has run a personal problem syndicated column in regional newspapers for fifteen years under the names, Barbara Boston, Molly Mason, Sandra Lee, Paula James and Cath Clark. She answers hundreds of letters each week. Here are some samples from people striving to deal with the aftermath of divorce, bereavement and other forms of loss.

Bereavement

Dear Barbara,

I was widowed two years ago and have been unable to pick up the pieces. I have become increasingly depressed and withdrawn – not fitting into any social situation, and now live a life of virtual isolation.

I've hit the very depths of despair on many occasions and it would have been a welcome relief if there had been no more tomorrows to face. I have a car, and a caravan on the coast, but these material things count for little when there is no-one else to share them with. This is a last ditch effort to surface again. Please can you help me? Where do

lonely people meet and make new friends? (I am 64 – and look 74.)
                                                                    Jane

This is the classic letter about loneliness following bereavement. Nothing matters any more. Two years of utter misery have passed since the death of a beloved husband. Yet, had this lady known it, her 'last ditch' effort was *because* about two years had elapsed. The mind and body need so much time to find release from the overwhelming shock and grief – but then make a positive 'pull' towards restoring some kind of normality. Jane's letter when published spoke its own message, and within days an avalanche of replies arrived for her, many of which began 'It could have been me writing'. If Jane wanted proof that there are hundreds of others sharing her experiences, she got it.

A subsequent letter from her, two months later tells a different story...

Dear Barbara,

I can't tell you what it has meant to receive the help and support from people all over the country since I wrote to you in desperation. Writing to an 'agony aunt' was the best thing I could have done. You have shown me clearly that there are many who care if only we will declare our need.
                                                                    Jane

Another reaction expressed by bereaved people is their disappointment when they counted on the support of former friends, only to find the response they receive quite different.

.....Life is very tricky for widows. The attitude of friends after a bereavement can be desperately upsetting. One couple I never visit now because the wife is 'politely hostile'. She thinks I'm after her husband, while another

couple I hesitate to contact because the husband made an advance to me – something he would never have thought of doing while my husband was alive. My family have been a marvellous support, but I want to be independent. It hurts so much that past friends let me down when I need them so much. Instead I am treated with suspicion or as fair game now I am alone. This, to me, is real loneliness – being pushed out of friendships that my husband and I enjoyed before.
                                                                    Mrs Smith

This lady may have read her friends' reaction correctly, she could also have been so over-sensitive that she misinterpreted it. The polite hostility could have been the reaction of a woman who just didn't know what to say, was embarrassed by talking about a dead friend, and opted out for fear of saying or doing the wrong thing. Many people don't know how to talk to a bereaved person.

If someone wants to talk about a dead partner let them, as the reciting of events leading up to the death and its aftermath is a form of release. The fact that the partner is alive in memory is a tribute to the relationship and a comfort to the survivor. In any case, don't avoid speaking about a deceased person.

In the second instance, the widow could have imagined that an arm round her shoulder or a squeeze of the hand was an 'advance' when it was in fact only sympathy. Even so, sexual harrassment is much more prevalent today generally than most people realise or admit.

Widows or widowers shouldn't shun former friends too quickly. Give them a chance as, in a bewildered state of shock and loneliness, you grope for help, and find that your friends may be shocked, unsure, fearful themselves, and not reacting, certainly for a while, how you hoped they might. A local branch of CRUSE or the National Association for Widows may also help you cope with your confused feelings (address on page 89).

False pride

Feelings of injustice, resentment or false pride can explode into a situation which is literally out of the frying pan into the fire.

.....I'm writing to you in sheer desperation as I feel so distressed and lonely after the break-up – instigated by me – of my 27-year-old marriage. We have two sons and a daughter, now grown up. I have always been a full-time housewife and mother. My husband is quiet and never went out much, until we joined an operatic society. He then became so heavily committed there that most of our evenings were taken up, and he wouldn't even go on holiday. Instead of talking the problem over I exploded into a violent temper and suggested we parted company. I also put our house on the market.

If only I had discussed my problems with someone instead of getting into a state, I would not have done something I now bitterly regret. We should be enjoying ourselves (we are both in our early 50s) together. Instead, we are both struggling to run separate homes. I am lost and empty.

Mrs L W

This lady's pride made her keep her problem to herself and led her to jettison a marriage she now feels could have been saved. Pride is not to be trusted. Saying sorry may be difficult, admitting to having problems you can't solve unaided may be anathema to a sensitive person, but it is a thousand times better than despair. To throw away in anger a friend, a partner, a relationship, can cause unimagined loneliness. Obsessive loyalty to any organisation at the expense of family and home can be taken too far. Val Marriott suggested that the lady talk to her husband, fully and without anger.

Family feuds

.....It is a year since my son and his wife told me they wanted nothing more to do with me. This was when I did not attend their Silver Wedding party as I did not feel well enough. I bought a gift, but they took it badly and won't come near me. I am a widow, crippled with arthritis and on my own. You can imagine how lonely I am. I had trouble with my son years ago – he got this girl pregnant at 16 and had to marry her. But that's forgotten now.

Mrs G

Someone has to make the first move in this rift, or it will go on, harder to heal, for many years. Mrs G should write to her son and daughter-in-law, showing she wants to be friends, is sincerely interested in their welfare, and is keen to bury the hatchet. She should continue to communicate even if response is slow. It seems that her non-appearance at the wedding party was taken as an indication that she considered their marriage no cause for celebration – it obviously re-opened old wounds.

Mrs G should also not brood too much, she needs friends of her own generation and interests so that the situation with her family does not get out of perspective. Being at peace with the family is what she should aim for, not sorting out who was, or was not, to blame.

Agoraphobia

Writing to an agony aunt can be the first step to dealing with a problem like agoraphobia – the fear not only of open spaces, but also of going out alone to take a walk or do the shopping.

> .....*I am an elderly widow and one of those people who cannot go out normally. I push myself, thinking 'I will make myself go out, and if I drop, someone will pick me up'; but it is wearing me down physically and mentally. I also have another worry: my little dog is now blind and deaf and very old. I feel I shall go to pieces completely if she dies, and it could happen any day. I have nowhere to go. My daughter lives miles away and I am unwanted by my son's wife. I even look forward to the gas or electricity bills coming through the door. What can I do?*
>
> *Lonely One*

After this letter was published in a local paper, over 100 replies from dog owners who lived in the same daily dread were forwarded to this woman. She was encouraged to contact the Open Door Association (address on page 95) for agoraphobics and received offers from the local support group to accompany her on shopping trips.

Being ill and alone

Terror of being ill and alone can strike at any time, as shown in this letter:

> .....*I am a woman in my 70s, living alone in a top flat. Neighbours do not speak. I attend my doctor's regularly for check-ups. But recently I was in a supermarket when I got a shooting pain in my left side. I have been in trouble*

with nerves for years, and I got in a right state of panic.

At the health centre I was given a prescription. I asked the pharmacist what it was and he said it was often prescribed for people with angina. The doctor never said I had angina – he said my heart was okay. I have no-one to talk to – I don't know if I'm dying – am scared to sleep, my heart keeps pounding away. I am so desperate, I have not eaten for days. *Flat 37*

Val suggested that this lady should write down the things she wanted to know, and take these questions straight to the doctor. In a surgery patients get so distraught they don't ask half the things that are bothering them.

Having no-one to confide in made health and death an obsessional worry for this woman whose doctor should have explained why the tablets were prescribed, and she should not have accepted the pharmacist's diagnosis as definitive because many drugs have several uses.

Allaying this woman's fears is essential. She, and many people like her, would benefit from regular calls from a volunteer visitor or by contact with a local support group for a particular illness, such as the Chest, Heart and Stroke Association (address on page 94). The woman could also have used the Samaritans 24-hour life-line in her moments of anxiety.

Access to grandchildren

Longing to find lost relatives can become an obsession for lonely older people as described in the following letter:

.....I am a grandmother living all alone. My one grandchild was only small when I last saw her, and I keep

wondering if she knows she has another Nana. My son's marriage broke up, and my daughter-in-law went off with everything. He tried every way he knew to find her. Years later she sent divorce papers from Canada, but the address turned out to be false.

Is there any way I can find out where my grand-daughter is before I die? I am getting on, and my thoughts are always with this child, taken from me before she was old enough to know me.
                                Lonely Nana

There are ways this woman could try in making contact: start by getting in touch with members of the daughter-in-law's family and asking them to forward a letter or give a contact address. After all the intervening years, any feelings of bitterness may have been forgotten. She could also try the Salvation Army's relative tracing service.

Legally the matter of grandparents having access to grandchildren is dealt with by a court order when the parents are separating or divorcing, or when the parents of the child are not married. For further information about access, contact Parents of Parents Eternal Triangle (address on page 92). Age Concern is also producing a book on the rights of grandparents, available in 1989 from the address on the inside back cover.

Second marriages

Gentleness and communication between partners is even more essential the 'second time around' than it is in first marriages.

.....My wife and I are now in our late 60s. It is a second marriage for us both – but life for me is desperate because my wife's daughter from her previous marriage can't live

*without having her mother round her neck all the time.
Every other week my wife goes off there for days at a
time. I cook and clean and wash and look after myself,
and feel I have no life (I am badly crippled with arthritis
and find great difficulty in walking about).*

*My wife has been away over a month now, and I'm at
my wits' end with unhappiness and isolation. It is obvious
she doesn't care for me as much as for her daughter. I feel
I could accept being alone more easily if she were dead – I
would know I had to find a solution to keep myself going.
But I'm stuck here with a hope that one day she just
might return. You see, I still love her.* Mr M E

This is another form of loneliness – the hoping against ever
fading hope. All this unhappy man can do is to force his wife
into a decision – to leave for good, or to understand the torment
she is causing and wriggle out of her daughter's apparently
vice-like grip.

Has this man ever said to his wife, 'I want you and I need
and love you. Please can we have some happy life together in
our years of retirement?' When his wife is at home, does he
constantly berate her for putting him second to her daughter?

Human nature being what it is, he probably does the latter.
But every problem has several sides and angles, and perhaps
gentleness has not figured in this second marriage sufficiently
on either side. It is best to think of your own faults as well as
your partner's, and to remember that people respond much
better to kindness and thoughtfulness than demands. Worst of
all is the feeling of being 'taken for granted'. Only discussion as
honestly and objectively as you can – admitting your own
failings – can prevent this getting out of hand. Loneliness
within a relationship is a very sad state of affairs indeed.

Isolating oneself

Try to analyse whether you may be keeping yourself to yourself when you need to make contact with other people.

> .....*I have just returned from another boring night out all alone. I am a 46-year-old man living in a bedsit. The others in the house are years younger than me and don't want to know. I get on well with workmates and we laugh and joke – they think I am the life and soul of the party. But then I go home and cry. What do you think of a man of my age crying with loneliness?*
>
> *I have lost what courage I had and dare not join a singles club or anything like that. I just long to put my arms around someone and tell them I love them. I am a stranger in this area – I came here to get work – but why does everyone keep strangers at a distance? A kind word, a smile, would mean so much.*
>
> *Very Lonely*

Loneliness causes this man to fantasise – for a woman literally 'dropping from the sky' to end the predicament he deliberately hides from his workmates. His attitude gives the impression he doesn't need social contacts. Outside his work he waits for someone to smile, extend a hand of friendship to him. But does he smile at them? A 'boring night out all alone' suggests he leans up against a bar somewhere, sending out 'defiant' vibes to all around: 'Don't be sorry for me', 'I can manage on my own' – and he gets left alone.

Bars and pubs are very lonely places for shy, anxious people. By joining a group of people interested in a particular hobby, this man would be much more likely to find someone to communicate with.

Should you be lonely?

Not everyone seems sympathetic to the plight of lonely people, and the following comments perhaps indicate that misery can appear to be an indulgence. Are you sure that you are not unwittingly creating the wrong impression?

Dear Barbara

An old woman complained about her loneliness and her family's neglect of her. Well, how much time did she spare in her busy years to dance attendance on her parents? She should be grateful she has a family – countless poor souls have nobody. Her family are in the throes of their busy years and have problems of their own without having to cope with the self-centred groanings of a sour-faced old witch. I'm pretty positive that if she showed a lively interest in their doings and greeted them with a bright smile instead of stony-faced complaints they might even enjoy visiting her.

Dr S

Before you decide that nothing can help you come to terms with loneliness, consider the help you may get from religion.

Dear Barbara

In my experience most areas have at least one beacon of hope and help for the lonely – the local church, especially if it's a welcoming one. Often there are weekday or evening meetings, from devotional sessions to social events for pensioners. Many religious organisations extend their concern into the community by running clubs, coffee and chat sessions specifically for lonely people. The family atmosphere of a truly friendly church can be unique.

Mr L

Breaking the **L**onely **P**attern

As a key to understanding loneliness and doing something positive to counteract it, you may need to analyse your blackest thoughts and the moments when circumstances made you feel a little better. Loneliness may be the barrier that is preventing you taking advantage of the help you most need – like the man who was so lonely that even when someone did come to his door to offer help and some· company, he found himself speaking curtly instead of accepting the offers. Then when the visitor had left and he was alone again, he felt overwhelmed about his isolation.

Although loneliness is common to many people, there is no common answer to dealing with it. Perhaps one of the routes suggested in this chapter may help you....

Work brings rewards

If you are using energy and effort to help yourself as well as other people to earn money or improve your surroundings, you will feel better. Jobs may be difficult to find, or you may be too old or disabled to obtain paid employment; but there are things within your scope. Never think of the multitude of things you cannot do: turn your thoughts to what you *can* do. Many people are able to concentrate on only one thing at a time, and this can be turned to advantage. While working, your depression and loneliness must recede for a time. So every day give yourself a task which does not permit you to get up in the morning with nothing planned for the long, long day ahead.

To set yourself a daily project is essential – not some impractical scheme way beyond your capabilities, but something useful that you pledge yourself to do before going to bed that night.

Never let a week pass without exercising your creative talents. You do not need to be a genius to create beauty in your garden, to write a story, the words for a hymn, to start to knit or sew something, paint your room a different colour, take up an interest in music again. Remember your schooldays – what were you good at then? Did you show a promise that somehow has never been fulfilled?

The clue to your potential – and whatever your age, you still have a potential – is hidden somewhere in your early years. Think back, then channel your discoveries forward to the day ahead. Instead of thinking of the rest of your life as meaningless, concentrate on using each day so that as you turn in for the night you can give yourself a pat on the back for whatever you have achieved.

Appearances matter

In the spirit of self-appraisal look at a photograph of yourself taken a year or so ago, or study your face in the mirror. Are you letting yourself go? Perhaps with too much time on your hands, or with no incentive to get out and mix with others, your former standards of self-esteem have slipped so that you are presenting a much less attractive person – in terms of looks and personality – to the world.

Don't go shopping without first checking your appearance – clothes, hair, and shoes. Set aside time each week for washing your hair or if you are a woman, to visit the hairdresser. It is easy to say that 'no-one knows or notices, or cares what I look like'. Maybe not at this moment – but *you* should care.

It matters that everyone should try to make the best of themselves. Each of us has gifts, looks and abilities which can be fostered and developed. And first impressions do count – to other people, if not to you. They label you as a smart, well-groomed person, or as someone who doesn't care.

Which image do you want to create? What you are aiming for at this first stage of determined effort (just to test if any of these ideas and theories work) is your first compliment. A smile directed at you, a word of admiration, a question, spells hope. Today is what matters, and you can't risk wasting it.

Learn body language

Apart from your facial expression – and what you say – the way you sit, walk, use your arms and legs say a lot about your real thoughts. Shy or unhappy, you walk with your head down. If you are scared that someone may ask you questions or try to engage you in conversation, you tend to cross your arms firmly across your chest. Nervous women cross their legs tightly or wind them around the legs of the chair. An anxious person often sits, apparently relaxed, but with fists clenched.

Next time you are in the library, look for a book on body language. The subject offers an insight into the human race and will help you assess you own mannerisms and those of people you encounter. Being aware of body language adds to understanding and communication, and can also be a good conversational subject.

Controlling shyness

This may be a lifelong problem which never entirely disappears but can be controlled. Is shyness the reason you feel isolated? Is it a long-standing trait, the aftermath of divorce, bereavement, the break-up of a relationship, or the arrival of retirement?

How easy it is to read snubs into simple remarks so that you think people don't want to know you. You also resent others laughing, and seeming to be content, going about in groups. 'Why should they be happy/healthy/married and not me?' you ask yourself. Don't despise yourself for such a reaction – at least it's positive. You know something is amiss with your life which makes you angry. Lethargy is your greatest enemy and the hardest to beat. Avoid getting into a routine which can offer nothing in fulfilment or involvement.

Do not wrap loneliness around you like a defensive cloak against the rest of the world – its apparent comfort is really only a handicap to your progress. The longer you stay cocooned, the more difficult it is to break away. Your face may be hiding countless sorrows and anxieties, but do not make the mistake of thinking that the rest of the population is brimming with confidence. Once you start to talk to anyone, you soon realise that they, too, have their worries. When you decide to fight against the miseries of isolation, and re-learn the art of communication, you've formed a life-line.

Targets are important, but do not make impossible demands on yourself, such as forcing yourself to go to a party where you do not know anyone. You will feel more secure on your home ground – so be content to take opportunities that fall within your present capabilities.

To avoid being caught on the hop and prey to paralysing self-conciousness when you encounter neighbours, aquaintances and people you would like to befriend, it is helpful to memorise some conversational ice-breakers:

• *Make your conversation as cheerful as possible* After saying 'Hello', try to add some comment such as 'You look well' or 'Lovely day isn't it?' If you smile as you speak, you change the tone of your voice and make it more attractive and likely to bring a warm response.

• *Be aware of any special features of the day* 'Isn't it grand to see the flags flying for the Queen's birthday' or 'You know spring's coming when you see swallows nesting under the eaves, don't you?'.

• *Ask questions* 'I haven't seen your sister around for a little while. Is she well?' or 'I'm new to this neighbourhood. Can you tell me the quickest way to the post office, please?'.

• *Be truthful* 'I get so lonely – it's lovely to meet someone to chat to,' or 'I'm sorry I haven't been to the W.I. lately. Since I've been on my own I find it difficult to mix easily. I wonder if I could go along with you next week, just until I feel a bit braver,' or 'I'd be so grateful if you'd give me a hand across the road'.

• *Offer to help* 'I'm on my way to the shops. Is there anything I can get for you at the same time?'.

• *Pay small compliments* 'I'm always glad to see you – you look so nice and cheerful'.

• *Be topical* Mention what you've read in the newspaper or heard on the news: 'I see they're planning to build a new community centre which will be useful for us, won't it?'. When referring to an item of news: 'It makes you count your blessings when you see the problems some people have.'

• *Encourage people to respond* Other people's attempts to start a conversation with you will wither unless you offer some encouragement. Smile at the postman, the milkman, a neighbour, a girl at the supermarket check- out, someone you pass in the street. It doesn't matter whether they respond, although most will instinctively smile back at you. What matters is that you are rediscovering your rusty smile and using it to face the world again.

Joining in

Perhaps you've never been a 'joiner', avoiding clubs and all organised groups. But you need this contact now. If you used to enjoy a hobby or interest, recultivate it. Loneliness saps energy, confidence and enterprise; but any small talent that is developed will bring self-respect and admiration from others.

The town hall, library or Citizen's Advice Bureau have lists of organisations in your area, with the name of the secretary. Don't force yourself to make your first visit to a group on your own. Contact the secretary beforehand, say you will be coming along, and ask to be introduced to a few people until you are comfortable. A common interest will make conversation easier, and a good group leader will get everyone so involved that shyness and inhibitions will be forgotten.

Whatever your particular interest or problem, there is usually a self-help group, like those listed on pages 87 – 102, dedicated to giving support and practical assistance. Accept offers of support gracefully, and eventually you may reach the point of feeling able to say 'It is my turn to help someone else now'.

Many valuable organisations – some nationally known, others purely local – survive on voluntary effort; and for many volunteers their commitment is their escape from loneliness. Anyone who offers time can be found a form of service to suit temperament and skills. Because voluntary organisations exist on friendly teamwork, someone giving his/her services gains access to an enlarged circle of people, in addition to those receiving the service. First, before 'signing on' for one particular organisation, it's a good idea to get a full picture of what voluntary opportunities are available.

If isolation has been thrust upon you because of some disability, be aware that for many physical and mental conditions there are self-help organisations which offer information as well as local support. Once you have made contact with people with expertise in dealing with a particular problem, you may be able to forget your worries about mixing with others especially if you suffer from rheumatism and arthritis, or agoraphobia or incontinence – just to name some of the most common complaints.

Once you understand the limitations of a disability, it is possible to find activities and pursuits which are within your capabilities, supported by the companionship of other people who understand the problem.

Strategies for breaking out

For either fit or disabled people, breaking out of loneliness requires individual strategy, as illustrated by the examples below. Do you identify with any of the people involved? Do the suggestions help you to get a different slant on your lifestyle?

Example

Mrs B is a widow in her 70s, living only on her pension. Her neighbours are younger, working people. She cannot walk far easily because of arthritis. She can only just manage to pay her way even with help from income support. How can she avoid loneliness and despair?

Strategies Has she contacted the local Age Concern or another organisation that runs a day centre or luncheon club nearby? What about membership in the local arthritis group which may organise meetings and outings as well as a transport scheme to take people to and from meetings?

One way to make contact with her young neighbours would be to ask if they could do with someone to keep an eye on their homes when they are at work or on holiday.

Has she family or friends living within reach? Has she told them about feeling lonely? Would they visit, or ask her to visit them, if they did know? – What about penfriends? Seeing the postman come to the door gives a big boost to self-respect and proves someone cares.

Example

Mr C is a widower also in his 70s. Since his wife died he has to fend for himself, which he hates. He is lonely but is unfriendly if anyone tries to help. He also worries about what will happen if he should become ill, and when his small capital (in the building society) dwindles to nothing.

Strategies Mr C can get about, if only he could bring himself to join a church, a men's afternoon club, or the retirement club of his old firm, or re-kindle an interest in a hobby or skill he used to enjoy.

He needs to rethink his attitude to others – opportunities are there but he is deliberately turning his back on them, or spurning overtures of friendship. He should make an effort to meet people half-way when they offer help.

It may be the right time for Mr C to consider sheltered housing. Within a warden-assisted scheme he would not feel so bereft. Probably there would be more women than men living there, and he would be sought after to help with small jobs – eg checking electrical plugs, unstopping a sink – that women sometimes need help with. This would make him realise he still had a purpose. He may also be missing the company of a woman more than he realises.

A local Age Concern group or the Citizen's Advice Bureau might have access to a financial adviser to explain the options available for people on small incomes, like a home annuity scheme. The Age Concern publications about housing and personal finance, listed on pages 103-4, should also be consulted in addition to a bank manager.

Mr C should make sure that he is eating balanced meals – though he may be eating enough, his diet may not include the right nutrients. Eating well does not mean having to spend more on food.

Example

Mr D is 56. He is unemployed, unmarried, shy and lives with his widowed mother. He has no friends and rarely goes out and is deeply lonely. He has never been able to form a satisfactory relationship with anyone other than his mother. Shyness and lack of self-esteem are his downfall and he needs to find something that he can do well – perhaps he is good with his hands or maybe he can cook. People who can offer such services are in demand.

Strategies Because he is unemployed he could work part-time at unsocial hours. He needs the involvement, the sense of belonging, a reason to get up in the mornings that a job brings, whether it's voluntary or paid. He must learn to rely on himself – the chances are that he has been 'mothered' and does not think of himself without reference to his mother. He could start by making a list of what he wants from life along with practical ways of achieving his aims.

Lethargy is an enemy and Mr D should make a real effort to keep fit. A rambling or cycling club would make few demands, socially, on a shy person like Mr D, but would get him together with others to participate as much as he wishes.

What could he do for other people? A fit and active man, has a lot to offer to voluntary work or in neighbourhood projects. Mr D could make friends through a genuine concern for others and by looking for someone he could befriend who needs him as much as he needs them.

Example

Ms A is a single parent with two small children, living in a small flat and on income support. She can't get out without taking the children with her, and she can't afford a baby-sitter. She has no friends, is desperately lonely and needs to think of ways to improve her situation.

Strategies She could join the local mother and toddler group where she'd meet other young mothers. One or two might also be single parents who would welcome getting together for company in the evenings. They could share baby-sitting between them with one of the women staying at home to look after all the children in one home, while two others could go out. They could also organise a group activity, perhaps a money making one, such as sewing or cooking.

During the day Ms A could do some job, such as being an Avon Lady, and take the children with her in the pushchair, which would of course be a way of meeting other people.

Looking ahead to the time when the children are at school, she could do a correspondence course to learn a skill to help get a job – remembering that there are concessions for people living on benefit for many courses. The local library or CAB should provide a wealth of information and books for planning careers.

Squaring up to Isolation

Even the famous, apparently awash with security and friends, can feel acutely alone. As the celebrities quoted in this chapter show, every person's story is different, although the experiences all echo the same theme: lonelines can be conquered with some help from the side-steps outlined on page 44.

How celebrities cope

Jimmy Greaves *My goal is stick together*
.....I certainly know what it is like to be lonely – to feel there is nothing left to live for. To be right at rock bottom... I have never been an extrovert. Even when I was playing football I was not 'one of the boys' – I found it difficult to communicate easily with people. It was easier after a few drinks. And so I began on the lethal combination of drinking vodka and beer which turned me into an alcoholic and demanded everything I had, including my life.

I would sit there, all alone, trying to sober up. I didn't want another drink because I knew it would plunge me down to even further depths, yet I could find no reason why I should sweat it out, through all the pain of not drinking, back to being sober and suffering even more because of what I had become.

Even now, I cannot say what power it was that came to give me strength to face the long upward haul to get out of alcoholism. Nor can I explain why some people find their way back and others don't. I just know that it taught me a million things I never knew before about myself and about other people.

I now speak out and take the consequences if I feel strongly about something – for there is far too much repression about. Natural emotions are stifled for fear of upsetting others, or admitting our own inadequacies. Diplomacy taken too far alienates people from each other because you never know who is speaking the whole truth. That is stupid, because members of the human race only have each other for survival, love and support, and we should be sticking together, not isolating ourselves through inhibitions.

Barbara Cartland *Find something to do*
.....There is no reason for anyone to be lonely if they work. As President of the National Association for Health, I have letters all the time from people who are ill because they have nothing to do.

What I say to everybody, especially to women who have either lost their husbands or who are alone and getting old, is to go to their local town halls who have a list of the organisations in their area. There are charities or political groups who are delighted to have people to help them, especially if they do not particularly want to be paid.

In this way you meet a great number of new people. When you have found which group you are happiest with, or where you make the most friends, you can drop the others.

I am 86 and wrote 24 books in 1987 and I am so busy I am wondering how I shall get through this year. This is what makes one happy and prevents one from feeling elderly. What is hopeless is to try to rely entirely on your family and friends to keep you amused. You have something individual to do yourself and there are masses of things one can do if one only takes the trouble to look for them. Also compassion, understanding and caring for other people in any way means that people come to you for advice and help as you get old; and young people love to talk to what to them is a 'grandmother' image – they just love someone who will listen.

It is after you have listened to other peoples' troubles that your experience, knowledge and expertise of life comes into real use because you are helping another human being.

Clare Francis *Loneliness is all to do with people .....Loneliness is not geographical – it is all to do with people. It is like New Year's Eve in a strange city with parties going on all around you to which you have not been invited. It is the feeling of being different.*

Being solitary, as I have been many times on my sea voyages, is a pleasurable sensation, not to be confused with loneliness. It is good to choose to be alone – you get things into perspective.

But a woman on her own has to realise there is no easy access to social life. You do not get invited to dinner parties, married couples give you a miss. At the end of a relationship, for whatever reason, previous friendships are largely lost to you.

These days it is considered smart to live alone, but I often wish we could return to the days of neighbourhood communities where people knew each other and talked.

I became ill a few years ago. Doctors and specialists told me there was nothing wrong with me. Friends at first urged me to 'pull myself together', then I got positive disbelief about any health problems. That was the ultimate in loneliness. I felt awful, as if I had a combination of 'flu and a hangover, and no one believed me!

It was only when my condition was finally diagnosed as ME (myalgic encephalomyelitis), and I started to organise a self-help group that I began to communicate with others who understood, because they too were sufferers from ME. I used to think you could beat anything, all on your own, by mental effort. I know now how wrong I was.

Ann Todd *Life is an adventure*
.....I believe so much in change. You should never, faced with a situation, sit down and say, 'I can't do it, I can't

cope, I'm so lonely' – for that situation has been sent to you with a purpose. To fail to use our time here, in a world which is a mixture of both good and evil (yet should always be exciting) is to deny destiny.

I am grateful for my life – I feel I have been very blessed and have always felt, somehow, guided. I am lucky to be an international film star who has worked with and met people who had and have a profound effect upon me. I now must be ready for what I have to do today and in the future. Life is an adventure and no one should permit themselves to be blown haphazardly through it, but should take opportunities, using whatever gifts have been given.

I believe most of all in love and courage. I have a blinding faith in God, knowing that when I feel lost and lonely I can cry for help and help will be given, so long as I, too, am prepared to give all my energies and faith to what is required of me.

I don't want to go to the next world as a 'new girl'! I want to have learned from this life so that I have a head start for what is to come... In fact I had a line I loved to say when I played Peter Pan – 'To die will be an awfully big adventure'.

Jimmy Savile *Climb every mountain*
.....Some years ago I was trapped three-quarters of the way up Ben Nevis, Britain's highest mountain. The 28 hours I spent on my own waiting for my colleague climbers was the ultimate in loneliness. Being different from most people I actually enjoyed it enormously. The fact that it

was fraught with danger bothered me not at all and 28 hours passed as slowly as a lifetime. Obviously loneliness is different to different people, but I don't find it at all unpleasant. In fact, I just might go back for a whole week.

On second thoughts, perhaps I'd rather opt for a warm desert island.

Barry Took *Never give up hope*
.....My loneliest days were when I was in my 20's. I was working as a stand-up comic, yet with an instinct that this was never going to be my true vocation! I was in a small company, touring endlessly from town to town, never having any roots anywhere. I was withdrawn – I could not mix with the others in the company. They were gregarious – happy to go to the pub and play snooker all day. This highlighted the fact that I was the 'odd man out'. I would wander the streets, miserable, aimless, wondering what to do with myself.

One day it was very cold and cheerless – I found myself standing, almost in desperation, in front of an art gallery. Admission was free – and what was more important to me at that moment, it was warm inside! I walked around, gazing in awe at the pictures and suddenly found myself feeling 'at home'. Everyone else was doing just the same as I was, and some of them spoke to me, asked questions, obviously regarding me as a like-minded person. It was a wonderful feeling. Everywhere I travelled after that, I sought out the art galleries, and inevitably, began to learn more, and read about art – a lifetime's interest had begun.

I discovered Rodin's Age of Bronze. Years later, when we married, my wife Lyn and I went on honeymoon to Paris and visited the Rodin Museum. Just one tiny moment of decision on a winter's afternoon in a northern town altered my entire outlook. From being a shy, unhappy , lonely young man I became a person who had something to think about, places to go to, and people to talk to. That's why I firmly believe that, however thick the web of loneliness may seem, there is always a way out, for everyone. So long as they never give up looking.

Dudley Moore *Work with patience and love*
.....For 17 years I suffered intense loneliness, all the time asking questions and going to analysts. When I finally allowed my vulnerability to show, the dividends were gigantic, and people responded immediately.

When you start to learn to enjoy life, you stop asking questions about it. You don't seek to know what its meaning may be, because the pleasure of each day is so great.

You have to learn to live with yourself, and give yourself a break and like yourself. I think you have to be prepared to work (to whatever end) with patience and love and not merely to beat yourself to death.

When I am at my lowest ebb, I look at myself and ask, 'What am I doing to myself which is causing this feeling'? Pressure is often caused by people doing what they don't want to do. They cannot analyse their own depressions, see what is creating them – and stop it. I can

*now – with much more perspicacity. I wouldn't want all
those previous years over again. I've learned to 'go with
who I am, and not fight it'.*

Side-steps for bad moments

For famous and ordinary people alike, the pangs of loneliness
can be sharp, and each person has to find a way out of the maze,
step by painful step. Think of moments you dread, of daily
ordeals when fear and desperation grip you. Possibly you can
side-step them by anticipating their effect:

Moment: The terror, sometimes mounting to panic, of
opening the front door and knowing that no one, no
welcoming presence, is inside.

Answer: Have a pet to welcome you or leave the radio and
a light on so that home does not seem so empty.

Moment: Finding a coffee cup from breakfast still in the sink
when returning home much later.

Answer: Wash the cup before going out to avoid being
reminded in this way of being on your own.

Moment: Going to bed alone.

Answer: Many lonely people make a ritual of going to bed by
staying up for the ten p.m news on TV, and when the
newcaster says 'Goodnight' they say the same – a small, but
comforting exchange. Having a nightlight also gives a
reassuring glow should you be wakeful.

Moment: Having news and no one to tell it to.

Answer: A telephone is a life-line, not just for an SOS but for
contacting an organisation like those listed on pages 87-102.
The phone is vital for chats with family or friends and also gives

you dial-a... access to everything from pop music to recipes.

Moment: Feeling out of place, almost an alien, in your street, to whom you are little more than 'that person at No.35'.

Answer: Make an effort to be on good terms with at least one person or family in the street. Apart from pleasantries and expressions of interest when you see them from time to time, they can be invaluable allies in an emergency.

Moment: Dreading your own birthday – because of the mocking, cardless mantelpiece.

Answer: Treat yourself to some item like a new picture or a bunch of flowers – that will make the day special to you however oblivious the rest of the world seems. Try tuning in to birthday greeting request-type programmes, many of them having their own version of a 'quiet' birthday to share with millions of others.

Moment: Looking around the living room and being bored by the same decor, books and pictures.

Answer: There are many possibilities for injecting new colour, character and 'feel' into a room, as explained in the chapter 'Make home say welcome'. If you need some new books to read and look at, libraries offer a wide selection of subjects and titles, and all for nothing. If you're someone with an interest in travel, crime, or sport, for example, there are book clubs which cater for particular subjects.

Have something new to hang on the walls. Posters are sold in a variety of outlets, and some libraries lend pictures, mainly of the Van Gogh and Chinese Girl vintage. An excellent way of seeing if a picture 'works' in your home before buying it is to try it out for a few months.

Moment: The onset of winter and inevitable retreat to what seems total social hibernation.

Answer: Side-step this by getting yourself to an evening

class. Start planning your next spring or summer holiday, not just by collecting brochures but by doing some background reading about the culture, food and wines of your intended destination. It also helps to learn some basic tourist phrases in the relevant language.

Moment: Feeling lost in a crowd, a floating 'anonymous' unit in a statistical ocean.

Answer: Sympathy and friendly feelings may not be obvious in the faces of others in that crowd, but if you trip, some hand will usually reach out to help you. Likewise, your smile will touch goodwill in someone else. Regard all people you meet positively, as potential well wishers to you, at least until proved otherwise.

Moment: Laying the table for one – an especially desolating ritual on birthdays and other festival days.

Answer: Setting extra places for imaginary guests just won't work, so if there's no chance of making up numbers, think small. Have your meal on a tray or at a smaller table than usual, complete with your best china so that the occasion is different for you whatever company you haven't got.

Moment: Drawing the curtains on a dark winter afternoon.

Answer: This should be the cue for turning on some cheering lighting and some extra warmth and reaching for a new 700-page novel that's far too long to tackle at any other season.

Moment: Worrying about money when it's raining bills.

Answer: If you've gone through your priorities and find the pound and pence picture still troubles you, it may be time to talk to the experts – a Citizens Advice Bureau, your bank manager, or write to one of the money advice columns that many daily papers now run.

Moment: Feeling confused in the supermarket and resorting to panic buying.

Answer: Choose your shopping time carefully and have a detailed list of intended purchases, grouped together much as they are in the store so that you proceed without any time-wasting backtracking. Ask a friend or neighbour to accompany you so that you pool your knowledge of the bargains and layout. If you're particularly needing a chat, patronise the smaller, corner shops even if they may be a little more expensive.

Moment: Wishing the local synagogue, temple or church – or its members – seemed more welcoming to someone such as you who hasn't been inside the place since Sunday school days, or a friend's wedding years ago.

Answer: Some buildings are forbidding and ininviting, mainly for architectural or siting reasons. The real test of a place of worship is in the fellowship of its members, so take the time to look carefully in your neighbourhood.

If you'd prefer not to go alone, a note or phone call to the leader of the congregation should bring response from someone to introduce you to other members. Whatever you do, fight against an 'I'm all right, I don't need anybody' attitude.

Moment: Reaching for alcohol, a cigarette, pep pill or any other kind of drug with the justification that these will blunt feelings of loneliness.

Answer: The regular use of drink or drugs to drown or mask sorrows is a self-delusion. Even though some drugs may provide temporary escape from the apparently uncaring, even hostile 'real world', the long-term effects are often devastating and dangerous, and invariably make life more difficult.

Moment: Finding, again, that you have been 'betrayed' by a horoscope reading. Yesterday's promise went sour overnight and today hasn't been wine and roses all the way.

Answer: Only very lucky people can afford to believe in their daily horoscopes. If you are alone and wretched, a horoscope that says your life will be transformed before nightfall by the advent of some wonderful happening only leads to inevitable despair. The odds against such a miracle are countless, especially when aimed at everyone born within a certain month of the year. If the horoscope predicts a bad time, this only adds to your general feeling of malaise – so where's the point? There comes a time when you have to learn to make your own luck. Beginning to believe in yourself is much safer than relying on any astrological patter.

Writing, Dating and Sex

Penfriends can be a regular, lively source of comfort and stimulation. Dating agencies too, can lead to happy endings. When did you last write a letter? And did you enjoy the experience? Was it a cosy chat with a friend or relative, almost as good as talking to them; or was it a chore, made up of boring half-details, spanning only a couple of pages?

'I'm no good at spelling' or 'I don't know what to say' or 'No one can read my writing' are the three most common excuses for not writing letters. But just seeing the postman stop at your door can more than recompense for having to sit down to write a letter in return.

Perhaps you have no one to write to – and no one who writes to you. Then you should consider belonging to one of the penfriendship clubs which bring so much pleasure to so many people (addresses on pages 97-98).

Getting down to writing

Think what you would like to know if you were receiving a letter from someone for the first time – the area where they live, their age group, and why they too have decided to make new friends through letter-writing. You would be hoping that the other person had some similar interests to yours, whether they enjoyed knitting, what TV programmes they watched, what organisations, clubs they belonged to. When you write to someone you don't know, remember to include some of these details 'to start the ball rolling'. A letter can provide a host of details about another person showing where your feelings and interests coincide.

Penfriendships can be long-lasting, like the one between a British woman and a New Zealander who began writing to each other when they were 10 and have grown to feel closer to each other than to many other people they talk to every day. They have shared so many experiences that they don't need to meet face to face. Photographs are regularly exchanged, and every Christmas they treat themselves to a telephone call to toast the friendship. The letters have been sad, happy, outpourings of anxiety or secrets that could be shared just because of the distance which divided them.

Many other people have found that letters can be a life-line in times of loneliness and despair, as well as joy when things are going well. It seems an effort to have to keep up a friendship when you're tired and very busy – the blank piece of paper may stare back at you for a while; but once you've started, you reach the end of the air letter before you've finished half you wanted to say.

Letter-writing is an art – but an easily acquired one – the main requirement being real interest in what other people will think when reading the letter. Here are two examples of letters which say more or less the same thing – but what a difference in the way they are written.

Dear Mary,

How are you? Full of aches and pains like me? There isn't much news, the weather has been so bad I can't get out. Most evenings I watch TV until bedtime, and often I think that's a lot of rubbish. I went to my ladies' meeting yesterday – only 10 turned up. Remember the times we used to have, when the children were all young – I wish things were the same now. I've nothing else to tell you. It would be nice to hear from you if you have a minute to spare.

Love, Elsie

Here is another version of the same letter:

Dear Mary,

How are you? Somebody asked me the other day, and I said 'Well, if I were a young woman I wouldn't want to feel the way I do now – but for an old'un I mustn't complain!' I can't get out much in the cold weather so I watch TV most evenings and try to switch channels so that I have a laugh or find something to make me think. The other night I actually shook my fist at some politician who was ranting on – good job there was no-one there to see me.

I went to my ladies' meeting yesterday. There were not many there but the speaker was talking about being part of the family. It reminded me of the times we used to have when the children were little. Do you remember the day we drove miles into the country for a picnic and when we got there I had forgotten to pack the food? I wasn't the most popular person in the world, was I? Even though I'm on my own now it's good to have memories for company. I always look forward to hearing from you – your letters are like having a chat together.

Love, Elsie

The second letter has exactly the same theme, but the writer has added a bit of humour and interest to the 'bones' of the letter, and there are a few subtle differences in the phrasing to give the words a human, friendly touch and encourage Mary to write back as soon as she can. The last sentence of the first letter: 'It would be nice to hear from you if you have a minute to spare' implies that Elsie doesn't expect Mary to find time immediately to reply.

So long as the story being recounted in the letter is readable, bad spelling doesn't matter. Messy writing does matter, for there is nothing more frustrating than receiving a letter you can't read. Either write more slowly, learn to print neatly, or buy an old typewriter. Nowadays secondhand manual typewriters are quite cheap, and you can teach yourself to type reasonably quickly with two fingers once you've mastered the keyboard sequence. Many older people find typing easier than holding a pen, especially if rheumatism in fingers is a problem.

Esperanto, the international language, makes it possible to communicate with people who live in many parts of the world, even if their native tongue is quite different from your own. The Esperanto Society runs courses and helps members get in touch with each other world-wide.

You can also correspond with tape-recorded messages. This is especially helpful to people who are disabled, and can't write easily, or are blind or partially sighted. Not only are there tapes available from the Talking Book Service for entertainment, but the same audio machine can also be used to record 'letters' to be sent to pen or tape friends for them to enjoy and respond to in the same way.

Even though a surprise letter or tape is lovely to receive, most lonely people prefer the predictable 'first of the month' offering. Such certainty implies discipline but, again, it's a shared 'duty' between you and your pen pal that surely makes it a lot easier.

Some topics to discuss

Small details of daily life – like shaking a fist at a politician on TV (or at the washing machine if it stops working, etc.) are all endearing human traits which add gentle spice to a letter. 'I've nothing else to tell you' is a really depressing thing to read. Either miss it out, or keep a diary with engagements or small comments jotted in it, so that when you come to write a letter you can refer to it.

Any of the following topics can add variety and colour to your letters:

Weather This is one of the great constant shared experiences of life, made better by saying how it directly affects your habits, activities and physical and mental state. It's the detail which makes such exchanges lively. Instead of 'hasn't it been awful?' explain how the conditions have been so bad that they've directly altered your routine, or forced you to call in a workman to mend the roof, repair burst pipes or a blown down fence. And – for good or bad – comment on the habits (punctuality, costs, standards, tea breaks, etc.) of the average workman. Everyone seems to have their own favourite horror story about pricey ripoffs, and fortunately, experience too of excellent workmanship and cheerful service.

Books Get used to keeping a short note about each book you read – 'racy story, wonderfully improbable characters, just right for a bedtime read for half an hour each night'. Or, 'not to be read in a lonely house in a howling gale, really scary'. Or, 'this author knows his onions – plenty of authentic detail and clever plotting to keep the reader on tenterhooks'. Armed with such 'crits', you can swop likes and dislikes with your correspondent. It may even help you to read each book more observantly and appreciatively.

Health Careful here, for there's only one thing worse than one's own feelings of depression, and that's wading through the woeful catalogue of someone else's pains, aches, anxieties and failed cures. Nevertheless, health too can be a subject of good humoured remarks – from the condition of the National Health Service to your own insights into medical matters.

Holidays Discussion of this subject may warrant special care, remembering the financial gulf that exists between the person heading for a fortnight in the sunny Med at the cost of several hundred pounds and someone forced to stay at home because just a weekend at a British resort would be straining resources. But don't duck the issue, share the fun/drama/pleasure of each break without necessarily dwelling on the cost or lavishness of it all.

Recipes These are an almost endless source of opinion and information to sweeten or savour your letters – with ethnic cooking increasingly popular, and the ingredients often inexpensive and widely available. Once you've tested a few 'winners', why not pass them on to a penfriend?

Gardening Everybody loves to see flowers and shrubs show signs of life, colour and fragrance. The size of the garden doesn't matter. Even a plot as modest as a few tubs or a window box is an activity worth enthusing about and for exchanging tips and ideas to help others, not to mention the appeal of vegetables as they become ready for picking.

Pets Many a dog or cat has had its antics described in enough detail to make up a book. Recording a pet's affection, funny ways or feeding habits should make you, as the owner, fonder still of yours and give food for thought as you struggle out in bad weather for the dog's daily walk.

A date with fate

For some people their contact with a penfriend lessens isolation, while others may want more emotional contact with a view to starting first a social, then a sexual, relationship. For these people a dating agency could be the answer to loneliness, so long as they understand what may be involved. Like the woman quoted below, however, many people wonder about the advisability of contacting a dating agency.

> .....*My husband walked out on me two years ago – and we are now divorced. I've tried to come to terms with going it alone, but I'm the sort of person who loves home-making and looking after someone. I shall never feel fulfilled without a man about the house. I would like to try a dating agency, but am scared that, at 55 I may be jumping from the frying pan into the fire.....*

An advertisement which says 'Find your perfect partner' may seem the answer to all the problems of loneliness; but 'perfect' and 'ideal' are two words which can deceive because they take no consideration of human frailties. Expect to find a perfect mate, and disillusionment will almost certainly follow. You must accept that you will have to make sacrifices and compromises if you commit yourself to sharing your life with someone else who probably has similar anxieties, inhibitions and communication problems.

Dateline, one of the largest agencies, does, however, point out that there are almost three times as many single woman over the age of 50 as there are men. This imbalance means that older women are unlikely to be swamped with possible partners, and introductions could be largely unsuitable. In many cases Dateline suggests that people try their magazine *Singles* which carries hundreds of personal advertisements every month.

There is unquestionably a great number of happy endings; but there is an equal number of people for whom dating agencies do not provide a mate and highlight loneliness, when they have paid dearly for introductions which have been failures. Although Dateline claims that their fee of £85 for a year's membership is less expensive than any comparable service, you may find there is a local dating agency whose fees are lower.

The distance involved in actually meeting a contact is one major hurdle in the 'matching' of members. The questionnaire to be filled in is comprehensive, and the data is fed into a computer which then comes up with the names of clients who may be a compatable match of pairs.

This assessment, it must be said, relies on clients telling the truth on their questionnaires. But the most suitable people may not live in the same area, and many clients feel misled when the dating agency can only offer them introductions to people who live miles away and have no transport.

Here are some points to remember when joining any dating agency:

● Avoid any agency which hides behind a box number address, as there's no way you can make personal contact. Genuine agencies are usually happy for prospective clients to visit their offices to see how the dating system operates.

● Beware of an agency which does not permit you to state a convenient area. The mention of 'local introductions' is too vague and allows the agency to use the excuse that there is no one who lives locally so they are sending you to other possible dates much further away.

● Do not pay further sums of money after the initial fee if you are still awaiting a suitable introduction.

• Be honest about your marital state, age, interests, etc. as the questionnaires are strictly confidential.

• Don't be put off by what you think 'people might say' if you want to join a dating agency. Just acquaint yourself with the facts and the possible options, and go ahead, with financial caution! Remember the likely problems of your age group and the statistics quoted above about single women over 50.

• Don't join an agency 'on the rebound' from a failed relationship or after bereavement. You need to be at peace with yourself before embarking on a new relationship or affair. It takes months to recover from a failed affair, approximately two years to get on an even keel again after a divorce, and at least that amount of time to readjust after bereavement. You stand a far better chance of establishing a new relationship if you get over the worst traumas of a previous one first.

Sexual encounters

The sexual anxieties felt by lonely people can become disturbing. The word lonely is equated with being without sex, and the prospect of spending a lifetime deprived of the love of a partner is very hard to bear. These are some problems expressed by people living alone:

> .....*I am a divorced woman of 45, and although my marriage was unhappy, I find that now, being alone, I miss sex. I have been indulging in masturbation but this makes me feel guilty, ashamed of my own weakness and worried in case I am abusing myself. Please help.....*
>
> *Mrs W*

Therapists and doctors agree that masturbation is harmless and no physical or mental harm is caused by engaging in any exercise to relieve the build-up of sexual tension and loneliness. Sex therapists advocate masturbation for unattached, disabled and lonely people as a source of human comfort which they should not be denied because they lack a partner or are unable to make love because of a physical disability. It is the myth that it is wrong, harmful – or even sinful – which causes people to suffer mental anguish.

Resuming sexual activity after a long period of abstinence also makes people anxious, as shown in this letter:

Dear Barbara

> *I have been a widower for 12 years and since my wife died have had no sexual intercourse. Now I am to marry a widow I have known since my schooldays. Both of us had extemely happy former marriages. Although our main reason for marrying is companionship I would like to re-establish a sexual relationship, and so would my wife-to-be. She is 68, I am two years older. After all these years of celibacy will I have become impotent?*
>
> *Mr A*

If this man and his wife-to-be are able to discuss sex without embarrassment, they should also be ready to stimulate and encourage each other. If his wife finds intercourse painful, she may need to use a vaginal lubricant, such as KY jelly, to avoid friction. The man may need his wife's experience in love-making to help him gain an erection and enjoy intercourse again. Despite any initial awkwardness, they should regard sex as a bonus to their relationship and not become tense or anxious if it does not work too well. Companionship and sharing and a sense of fun, rather than sexual tests should dominate their life together.

> *.....My husband is getting on a bit and I am worried about us continuing to have sex. I've heard it could give him a*

heart attack, and I get so uptight I can't enjoy sex any more and would rather not try. Yet I'm lonely without that kind of closeness.....

The advice to older men and woman regarding sex is 'If you don't want to lose it – use it!' Even to people who have had a heart attack, doctors advise a return to love-making as soon as the patient feels the urge to do so. Don't deprive yourself of a close, loving relationship through false fears. Cuddling, kissing, touching and sex are by no means the prerogative of the young. A general rule is – if a person has a desire for sex – it won't hurt him/her. So relax and enjoy the experience.

Many problems are also experienced by homosexuals who have been in a long-term relationship. Their sense of loss when a partner dies or leaves them is acute, and frequently they get neither support not understanding from their families. It is essential to talk to someone who does understand – The Gay Bereavement project was set up to give support to homosexual people on the death of a partner (address and phone contact on page 89)

Making Home Say Welcome

Lonely people often lack a sense of belonging – of ever feeling 'at home'. For them the four walls around them speak only of what was or what might have been....

What kind of home have you created for yourself? It must be efficient so that running costs are affordable, but this does not mean it cannot be cosy. Don't be over fussy so that your home is more like a museum than somewhere to relax. Beginning at the front door, it can send out an unmistakeable message of welcome – even to you.

Creating welcoming messages

That message can be conveyed in many inexpensive ways: a light outside the front door at night; curtains that are open to the light and air, not drawn forbiddingly three-quarters of the way across the windows; a brightly-coloured rug before the fireplace; a vase of flowers on the table; a picture or ornament placed just where it catches the glow from the sun or a lamp; old cushions re-covered in remnants of quality fabric bought cheaply in the market – these are the imaginative touches that can set off a room, and lift your spirits.

Once you get started, you've jumped the main hurdle – for interest will be kindled as you see the improvement, and realise you *can* make even the most unprepossessing accommodation look welcoming. One thing you have plenty of is time – so why not slip in at the back of a local auction room, roam around a local charity shop, take your chance with the bargain-hunters at a jumble sale? You might find just the 'treasure' you need, and home is more interesting if you can look around and remember the story behind each piece of furniture or decoration.

Here are some key words, with suggestions to help you to make the most of your home:

Atmosphere Ideally your home should represent your personality at its most relaxed, created to lessen your stress and anxiety by its harmonious effect. Patterns and shapes should sit easily with each other, so that there are no jarring colours or angular items of furniture crowded together – but neither should your room look dull and predictable.

Have your radio handy to turn on when you first come in the door, so that total silence is avoided. Leave a piece of sewing, a half-finished crossword or jigsaw around. They give the room a 'lived-in' look and provide you with a sense of purpose.

Go ahead and use bold colours if you wish – asserting yourself by painting the kitchen in some brilliant shade may relieve bottled-up tension, as can scrubbing a floor, cleaning windows, or kneading your own home-made bread. This outlet of physical energy is necessary to help dissipate anger, frustration and fear, often caused by loneliness. Once you start to work towards making your home a place to reflect your ideas, you have banished that 'empty shell' that aggravates unhappiness, and you will create a more soothing atmosphere around you.

Your bedroom, kitchen, bathroom and living room should each look as if you cared about its appearance, and took the trouble to make it convenient, comfortable and clean.

Don't forget the importance of scent: pot-pouris, and perfumed candles, a lavender bag, or spray polish sweeten a room, even though the most welcoming smells are said to be fresh baked bread and percolating coffee.

Colours These have their own 'vibes', never more strongly than in your home. If you want to learn more, get a book on colour psychology from the library. Oranges and reds are 'quick' colours, attracting the eye instantly, whereas grey is a sombre background colour. Yellow is invigorating and can be beneficial to nervous people. Some colours will have a natural appeal for you – so use them, for you have never needed their stimulation more. Lighting, too, is important – once the curtains are drawn and you are settled, you want a mellow glow rather than a harsh white light to enhance your chosen colour scheme.

Focal points At one time the focus for a room was the fireplace, with chairs turned towards the flames. Nowadays a focal point may have to be created, perhaps with something red – poppies in a vase, a bowl of rosy apples, bright place mats on a table. Think of how you can give your room a feature to attract attention and add warmth and colour.

What if a room is dominated by an unattractive pipe or radiator, a damp patch or stains on the wall? That's when you need to exercise your ingenuity to disguise, cover or camouflage. Why should you put up with things you dislike? It is both positive and creative to do your best to get rid of them. A stained patch of wall can be camouflaged with a poster or a picture.

A few homely souvenirs can also act as a focus, cheer you

and start a new interest. Few people can afford to collect real antiques, but beer mats, books of matches or Victoriana can be the basis of a small display in your living room – and give you a reason to visit local junk shops.

Try to avoid having dark, heavy furniture as a focal point, for you won't be able to move the pieces around easily to alter the look of the room (or even for cleaning purposes). Smaller, lighter furniture gives you a chance to make changes, or move your chair nearer the fire in winter or to the window in summer.

Lighting The effect lighting can have on your mood is surprising, so make sure you have the most suitable lighting for each activity. An angle lamp over the back of your chair makes reading more relaxing, a low light is best for watching television, a standard lamp left on while you are out ensures that on your return the room is not dark and inhospitable.

Accent your best items of furniture, or a photograph by spot lighting, and perhaps use a dimmer switch in the bedroom to save electricity, yet leave a little light on all night in case you wake. The kitchen and hallways should be the brightest lit areas of your home, for safety reasons.

Floor coverings The effect of these on sound in your home is important. On carpet you won't notice the sound of your own footsteps as much – a sad sound which highlights your loneliness. Carpets give a warmer look to the room, and you should aim to treat yourself to a few creature comforts. When you are lonely you need to look for ways to be kind to yourself, when often the temptation is not to bother because 'nothing matters'.

Rugs cover up worn patches on the floor and give a bright look to a room – but when you are alone, safety is the vital factor. Care must be taken to avoid trips and falls – so rugs must not be put down on polished floors, and there should be no trailing threads or turned-up corners to invite accidents. You can buy sticky tape to anchor rugs and avoid them 'creeping'.

Mirrors These should be rationed, as too many reflections emphasise your isolation, but you can use a mirror to add light or to make a small area more spacious. Try to have a full-length mirror on a wardrobe door or attached to the bedroom wall, so that you check your appearance before going out. Or you could practice your smile, and take an analytical look at the way you look, walk and stand. Are you the sort of person who attracts others? How could you improve that image you see reflected in your mirror?

The Garden If you have a garden, it will sometimes fill you with dismay that there is so much work to do, for which you cannot find any enthusiasm. There will also be times when you cannot fail to be enriched by the wonder of flowers and plants. Just the act of sprinkling a seed packet of annuals – scented stocks, marigolds or forget-me-nots – holds the promise that very soon you will have a riot of colour to inspire you to become a more dedicated gardener, and plan flower, herb and vegetable areas.

The garden might also be your first contact with a neighbour to offer surplus vegetables, a bunch of flowers or some herbs over the fence – not to mention other gardeners who seeing someone tending their plants will offer advice.

Plants Even if you have no outside plot you can bring the garden indoors by having potted shrubs and flowering plants all year round. Geraniums will flower all summer, and if you take cuttings and re-pot them (carefully watering and feeding as well) they should survive the winter and be ready to give you more pleasure the following season. A young tree in a pot by the living room window gives the effect of a garden; and a hanging basket outside the front room window or door will add a welcoming touch.

A small porch makes an ideal greenhouse for propagating plants such as begonias or cyclamen, and you could try to arrange that you are never without a living plant in your room. Do follow the instructions for siting plants in shade or sunlight and for watering – otherwise you will be discouraged when they fail to flourish.

Adding a pet to your scheme

A dog's wagging tail, a cat's purr or a budgie's chatter will also add to the welcome of your home, not to mention the company provided. Fortunately, the domestic pet range is wide enough to ensure that even the smallest, highest flat is suitable for some kind of animal or bird, which could be so unobtrusive as to prevent even the most noise-sensitive neighbours from objecting.

Even though nowadays there are fewer restrictions about pet ownership in most rented and sheltered accommodation, you should find out beforehand just what they are – for it is heartbreaking to have to part with a much-loved animal.

Reasons for pet ownership are powerful: the warm, responsive friendship of a dog or affectionate cat, and the imposition of a daily discipline on the owner, implicit in the 'feed me, walk me, stroke me, talk to me' relationship. This provides someone else to think about besides yourself, and induces a more peaceful frame of mind which can also promote better health and even reduce blood pressure. The common remark 'I don't know what I'd do without him' is surely a testimony to the love and loyalty of an animal companion.

In addition cats and dogs have their own way of helping

their owners to make friends – with neighbours, with other pet-lovers or at a dog training classes where you learn together. Animals rarely equal humans in bad temper, and frequently excel them in trust and tolerance. Another factor for potential dog-owners is security. Even a small dog can alert you or a neighbour, or alarm a would-be intruder.

Whatever creature you want to share your home with – and remember that you'll be sharing *their* home once they get established – first discuss it fully with an expert if you don't know another owner. If in doubt over a technical point, consult the People's Dispensary for Sick Animals or the Royal Society for the Prevention of Cruelty to Animals (see addresses on page 100).

Sadly, many elderly people or those in poor health will not take on a pet for fear of dying and leaving it. A strong counter-argument to this fear is that pet owners often live longer and can make special arrangements for surviving pets, with friends, or through an animal aid group like the Cinnamon Trust or the Battersea Dogs Home (addresses on pages 98-99).

In weighing up the prospects for keeping the kind of pet you fancy, you must of course consider the practical points of space, time for daily walks or grooming, feeding costs, possible allergies (fur and feathers can irritate some people), noise and smell and how often you may be away on holiday or at work. Obviously, a pet must be appropriate to your means and routine.

Making the right choice

Here are some details to remember when choosing a pet for the first time:

Dogs Though they are generally companionable and responsive, you must take the lead. A dog will need to be vaccinated before it can go out in the street, will need a collar with your name and address, will rely on you to impose road and public place discipline, and for the daily rituals, periodic grooming and health checks. From the outset be sure you are taking on a dog you can comfortably accommodate, afford and handle – puppies can become vigorously strong in adulthood. Feeding a sizeable dog is not cheap either. The 'odd scrap' mentality won't do, as dogs need a balanced diet.

Cats They have a charm and personality all their own, but while less demanding than dogs – no walks, smaller appetites – they still need regular supervision to ensure happiness and health. Easy access to a garden or outdoor area is essential.

Budgerigars and canaries Budgies are the most popular pet birds, and their main needs are a suitable cage, a reliable supply of good quality seed (mainly canary and millet seed), regularly replenished water and some exercise (if possible free flying).

Canaries have an 'elite' – special breeds or varieties, often kept for show purposes. The needs of the 'basic' canary, which lives for about five years are similar to those of a budgie. If you are thinking of having a pair of canaries, avoid getting two cock birds, for they will fight. A local canary breeders club will be a useful source of information for the novice owner.

Tropical fish These are cheap to buy if you stick with guppies and neons, but it is easy to be tempted upmarket by exotic looking fish. Alas, they can be shortlived residents in your tank. The basic cost for a tank for cold water or tropical fish is about £30, plus oxygenating plants, tapwater conditioner, vacuum for cleaning the tank bed and filter. And for tropical fish, constant heat, at a few pence a day, is a must. All fish require a balanced diet and a regularly cleaned tank.

As not all of them co-exist peacefully, check before any purchase. Perhaps you would feel more at ease with a couple of goldfish – so long as they are happily accommodated in a large enough tank or bowl.

Maintaining your home

Grants and loans What happens if, inspite of all your efforts to make your home cosy and comfortable, you find it impossible to continue living alone; or your flat or house becomes too expensive to run? Are you aware of the various grants available to help with repair work and improvements for home-owners on low incomes, especially for older and disabled people?

Availablity of these grants varies between different areas of the country. A home built before 1919 might merit a grant for repairing foundations or the roof, for instance. There are also grants to cover the cost of materials for loft insulation; but do remember that you will need to get approval from the local authority before proceeding with the work. If you think the time may come when you have to care for an elderly or disabled person in your home, there are also grants available for adapting housing.

If you find there is no help available from a local authority grant for repair work, you might decide to opt for an interest-only loan (or maturity loan) mainly available from some building societies. These differ from ordinary loans as the capital is not paid off until the property is eventually sold.

Sharing your home When living alone is a problem, both financially and physically, it may be worth considering sharing your home with someone. Before taking such a step, however, it is vital to obtain the fullest possible professional advice. Such factors as use of space, the financial arrangements and the legal rights of each party must be considered – not to forget the commitment required from everyone involved to make the arrangement work. If sharing a home fails, it could leave you more depressed and lonely than before; but if it succeeds the benefits could be considerable. For more details about sharing accommodation, see *Sharing Your Home* listed on page 104.

Home security However modest your home, to be burgled is both a material and emotional disaster, even though the contents are fully insured. Some items cannot be replaced by money. So it is worth taking advantage of all the help offered to ensure that your home and contents are safeguarded. The local Crime Prevention Officer can give advice and point out potential fire hazards (there are free leaflets available from your local police station), and many areas operate a Neighbourhood Watch Scheme to deter burglars. This has advantages because a person living alone has neighbours to contact in an emergency, or to keep an eye on their home when they are away, and can offer the same kind of vigilance in return.

There are also alarm systems for installation within the home, and a further aid to safe living are smoke alarm systems which give immediate warning of any fire danger. More information on housing problems for older people living alone is given in the further reading section on pages 103-4.

Holidays and Sports

A holiday on your own

When you are lonely, a holiday is what you yearn for, to get you out of an isolated rut, but the thought of it may scare you to death. A holiday demands that you talk to other people or else sit like an outsider at a party away from the fun. How will you manage to go down to meals on your own to a table for one or a communal table where you are convinced everyone else will be talking to each other – except you? Such worries may haunt and defeat you before you even get to the door of the travel agency. But surprises could be in store, as many people will testify – like one widow who braved a holiday alone and later wrote down her experience:

> .....I was a nervous person and had always depended on my husband for company and a reason for living, as we had not had children. After my husband died I had spent a dreadful winter alone – my first experience of taking responsibility or coping without someone to tell me what to do. In the spring a nephew gave me a ticket for a coach holiday in the Lake District – an area I always longed to visit. But I was in a panic – I would offend my nephew

by not going but could I risk the embarrassment and loneliness of a crowd?

The deciding factor was that my husband had been a thrifty man, who would turn in his grave if he knew I wasted money already spent on a holiday. So I went, in trepidation and alarm.

When my nephew visited a couple of weeks after we returned from the Lakes, I gave him the details of how much I had enjoyed myself – beautiful scenery, kind people who had spoken to me, and a thoughtful courier who had made sure no one was left alone. It had been quite different from what I had imagined, and yes, I would like to go again another year. On my mantelpiece he noticed a small silver cup. When he asked me whether it was a prize for some achievement, I had to admit that I had won it for being the person who was always on the noisiest table at dinner time in the Lake District.

Mrs B

That woman's experience illustrates the importance of choosing a suitable holiday where other people are also on their own – perhaps a hobby or special activity holiday which encourages those with similar creative or sporting interests to mix naturally, or where there is a courier to make those first awkward introductions. No one ever needs to feel out of things, and some feel free enough – in the right group – to make a lively contribution to holiday meals and activities.

Many firms like those listed on pages 96-7 organise holidays with the single traveller as a top priority. Ask your travel agent to help you, and browse through brochures yourself to discover the holidays noted as being ideal for those on their own. Holidaying alone need not be hard work, but until you have taken the plunge and tried one, how can you possibly form an opinion? You will soon find out just how many other people are in a similar situation, eager for your company to swap experiences, to enjoy conversation and companionship.

The important points to remember are: that a single-person supplement on a hotel room may not be required when you travel with a specialist firm; that if you try, you will find a holiday to suit your ideas and your budget; that if you are able to travel at any time of the year, the choice is wide and you could find a real bargain.

Taking a winter break

The first experience of a holiday on your own may lead you to consider taking a winter break abroad. From December to the end of March when people on their own are so restricted by cold weather and long evenings, you could spend six weeks or more away in Majorca or one of the resorts in mainland Spain – thereby reducing your worries about weather, heavy heating and lighting bills, not to mention a rebate on car tax for every month it's off the road and a 'laid-up' reduction on accident insurance policies.

British Telecom will reduce rental charges if notified beforehand, and water rates can be cut by having the supply disconnected for the duration. Check first, though, that disconnection/reconnection is really worthwhile. And of course if your central heating uses radiators, the water supply must stay on if you want even minimal warmth there during your absence. If you rent a TV set or video, you can send it back for three months.

If the break is more than three months, the DHSS will arrange for your pension to be paid to you abroad, or the money can be paid directly into a UK bank or building society. Or you can let the pension orders accumulate, but remember that after two years they become invalid. While away, you can use travellers' cheques, or arrange for your bank to send a regular draft from the UK for cashing locally.

Another saving to be made while you're taking a winter break could be that your home earns its keep as a holiday base for visitors, but such an arrangement is best done via an agent. Whether you let your home or not, deposit valuables and money in a safe or the bank while you're away.

Sports for all

Unlike a holiday, taking part in some sport can be a regular activity as well as a way to make friends. Of course long distance running can be lonely, but most sports involve an individual pitting skill and stamina in the company of others – from just one other person to thousands in the London Marathon. Ask any rugby, hockey or squash players what they most enjoy about their sport and the answer is certain to include both the on-pitch or court battle and the post-game drink.

You can be as intense about a sport as you like, but may just want to join in for the fun. Don't, however, be casual in adjusting to the physical demands. However fit you feel, have a check-over from your doctor to be sure about blood pressure and general ability to cope with the strains of a particular discipline so that you can build up strength gradually to more energetic involvement. Heart, lungs and limbs all benefit from regular exercise.

Having summed up your physical strengths and weaknesses, and the availability of local facilities, give your chosen activities a fair trial for a few weeks at least. To reach a reasonable standard in some sports can take years, but many newcomers to something like jogging gain a real sense of satisfaction after the first couple of weeks of regular sessions. You may find an extra spur from keeping a 'progress diary' to mark your improvement. Be comfortable with what you attempt, and remember that exercise brings some risk of strain on joints and muscles. Joggers, for instance, are prone to ankle and knee damage if they overdo the distance or wear unsuitable footwear.

Fitness and relaxation The popularity of local authority classes or small exercise sessions in the village hall or someone's front room is proof of the need for such activities. Included in the general description of 'fitness/relaxation' are keep fit, yoga, all kinds of dancing from sequence to ballroom, modern, old-time and square, and of course the very popular tea-dance. Try at least one session of any activity you choose before committing yourself financially to a course of lessons. Once you have joined, you'll get great rewards by following the instructor's home exercise routine to keep in trim between classes and extend your capabilities.

Any form of exercise improves body control and breathing. If you are having an unhappy, lonely day at home, make yourself do a few exercises. Arm circling, bending and swinging your legs are excellent for getting circulation moving, and for losing that lethargic feeling. The experts suggest these general guidelines for exercise:

• *Get moving* Find a more active way to do your household chores and gardening activities, and use a greater range of movements for a longer time.

• *Gradual build-up* As it takes time to get fit, you'll experience more breathlessness and sweating than you might have expected. Warm up first with easy bends and stretches; after vigorous exercise, ease down with a slow walk for a minute or two.

● *Basic fitness* This comes from regular exercising, so be prepared to give up to a minimum of, say, 30 minutes, two or three times a week. Even chronic conditions or a tendency to sprains can be reduced by a steady build-up of muscle strength from regular exercise.

Fitness once attained, is the ideal springboard for moving from general exercise classes into more specialised sports – if you want to, but there should be no pressure on anyone to do more than they wish.

Bowls This is among the most sociable games – and you don't have to wear immaculate cream gear to play. Although beloved of pensioners, bowls is increasingly drawing in younger people as well who realise that as a test of hand/eye co-ordination it ranks with any other sport. Bowls is not over-energetic, and can be played indoors or out thanks to the increasing numbers of greens and rinks.

Cycling This enables you to get a change of scene as well as exercise. Instead of making it a lonely pursuit, why not join a club? You'll have company, a safeguard if anything goes wrong with your bike, and the club's leaders will have found the best and safest routes. Of course there are competitive cyclists, keen on breaking speed records, but there are also many club members who prefer a gentle cycle for a day's outing or a weekend trip.

Golf This is one of the great all-age sports, ideal for the person wanting a four-to-five-mile walk, a challenge, and ample chance for conversation. Swinging the clubs, and carrying them between holes can be quite tiring, so it's advisable first to try some rounds on a local authority course, with hired clubs, or to practice on a driving range. Later you can get a season ticket or join a club, though this is not cheap.

Jogging This is the slowest pace you can run and a good way to get your heart, lungs and legs used to working. You could start by walking briskly for ten minutes or try going up and down stairs without stopping for two minutes. If you don't find that exhausting, try walking and jogging for fixed distances. Don't jog until you are tired and then walk – keep the tempo easy and relaxed. The object is to pace yourself.

You may prefer to increase the jogging time and cut down the walking. Above all persevere, aiming to get out at least three times a week. Within six months you should see an improvement in both your general condition and mental well-being. As strength and speed increase, you may graduate to fun runs and marathons. Plan your schedule and your route, and you'll soon find someone of similar pace and ambition to jog with, which can be more fun and safer for you both.

Sports for disabled people The range of opportunities is very varied and challenging from the paraplegics' Olympics to local clubs which provide facilities for people whether they are paralysed, spastic, limbless, blind, deaf or mentally handicapped (see pages 100-101 for details of relevant organisations).

Swimming People can start to swim at any age and enjoy its benefits. If you are overweight, have back problems, or are stiff, swimming will suit you well, for it gives a feeling of weightlessness, as well as stimulating heart and lungs.

Having located your nearest pool, you would be sensible not to try to 'go it alone' but instead to take organised instruction at special sessions, perhaps for adults only, the over-50s, or disabled people – as your situation demands. It might be a good idea at first to pay a 'spectator' rate, and watch how the classes are conducted and the kind of people who are learning to swim – you will be reassured to see that they are no better than you are likely to be, yet are having a good time splashing about.

For anyone who is nervous about joining a class, a letter or telephone call to the instructor will result in your being met, introduced to other beginners, and encouraged to 'have a go', to avoid feelings of self-consciousness. A newcomer should find it easy to chat to others in the shallow end of the pool, all struggling to keep afloat, but with each other's support (both physical and vocal) progress will be made and a skilled instructor will help beginners to advance down the pool into deeper water. Swimming is an all year fitness aid, invigorating in winter and refreshing in summer.

Walking This is a popular way to make friends – just fall into step with one of the local walking or rambling clubs, which most weekends head for a scenic location. The pace won't be frantic, and the only required equipment is comfortable clothes, an anorak or plastic mac and sturdy shoes or walking boots, ideally 'broken in' before any long treks.

Arts, Crafts and Pastimes

Using time for a purpose

How often do you think to yourself, 'I ought to be doing something – get myself motivated' – but the effort required to get out and talk to other people is more than you can muster. Then perhaps, this is the time to begin some home activity which will at least engage your energy and concentration. Use it as both an interest and a stepping-stone to learning a skill or becoming more socially involved.

Don't drive yourself too hard – some days you will be able to achieve much more than others, but if you keep some unfinished hobby or pastime handy, there will be moments when you can whip up some kind of enthusiasm to 'have a go'. The process is accumulative – the first stirrings of interest can develop into really worthwhile ways to occupy your time alone.

Many lonely people say that late afternoon is their most depressing time, when they imagine everyone else is hurrying home to a family supper. The shops are closing, the evening looms interminably, and there is an aching vacuum. A diversion is urgently needed!

You only have to look on your library shelves to see rows of books on all kinds of arts and crafts, from basket weaving to wood carving. Some handicrafts do, however, need months of practice before a good standard of work can be produced, and failure to achieve some kind of success can be a real 'turn off'.

If you were never much good with your hands, why should the fact that you are alone and fed up miraculously make you deft? Only consider pastimes you feel naturally drawn to, and don't expect too much of yourself for a start. Group activities and classes are a great help where you will find others of a similar standard to yourself, and you can encourage each other in moments of frustration. Many classes are held during daylight hours, so there is no anxiety about going out alone at night.

The libary, town hall or local college will have a complete list of classes, and there may also be a transport service in rural areas for those unable to make a journey, particularly during winter months. There are plenty of 'beginner' classes, so there is no fear of your not being as good as the rest.

If none of the pastimes outlined below appeals, do not feel resentful – as if you are being forced into some activity which other people think is good for you, but for which you have little enthusiasm. Instead try to think of the possible advantages:

● You have too much time on your hands for brooding, and you really long to mix with people on an easy-going basis. Shared hobbies and interests offer a good chance to meet others with similar interests.

● You also want something to look forward to, a challenge which is within your capabilities once you put your heart and soul into it. If you find some activity – physical, mental or practical – that provides interest, friendship, and purpose, your life could be enriched in a deeper way.

A wealth of activities

Here are just a few suggestions of pastimes, most of which bring you into contact with other people:

Crosswords and Patience These are strictly activities for one, but they are ways of keeping both memory and concentration in good form. They are 'stimulators' because you need to think, to keep your mental processes active, and while you are working out a clue, or playing any one of the various games of Patience, you are not dwelling on your isolation – you are far too busy thinking.

Drama The last thing you may consider possible for a lonely person is to have to cavort about some stage! But for every person performing in front of an audience, there are several behind the scenes, organising props, prompting the actors, moving scenery making tea or helping with the costumes.

To be part of a team, presenting entertainment for a charity benefit or local theatre group gives a sense of belonging. Why not contact your local drama society?

Flower arranging If you have always enjoyed flowers, why not join a flower arranging class? There are so many techniques for transforming a few flowers, sprigs of foliage and an oasis-base into an artistic display. There are also competitions, where participants use their skills to illustrate book titles, seasonal themes, etc.

Knitting and sewing For many women (and an increasing number of men) these are two obvious creative activities. Knitting is rhythmic, soothing, and results in an 'end product' which you can wear yourself, give to family and friends; or you could find yourself in demand to knit for profit – for not everyone has either time or talent for such a hobby. A small advertisement (using a box number) in a local newsagents' window might produce enquiries and orders. Sewing, too, is a skill that is always in demand. If you can do alterations or make clothes, you have a potential 'cottage industry' – making anything from soft toys, to doing alterations for a local dress shop.

Knitting and sewing may not seem like career skills, but they provide lots of people with a purpose, a way of making some money as well as contact with other people. It is a boost to confidence if someone is eager to pay for some service you offer.

Making a scrapbook Among your treasures there is bound to be a pile of old photographs, newspaper cuttings about births, deaths and marriages and a variety of oddments relating to your family or local events. Why not put them in order and identify all the people you know in old pictures? It will bring back memories, and provide a real source of interest for your visitors. If at any time in the future you have to move, your family history book can go along with you for company. There will be items to add from time to time as well. Or you may find yourself interested in your family tree, tracing back through several generations. The local registrar of births, deaths and marriages, and parish records may reveal all kinds of details about unknown or lost relatives.

Music You might never have the nerve to sing on your own, but how about becoming a member of a choir or music group? If you can carry a tune, you will be welcome by a church or male voice choir or by a mixed group. Many people find singing a therapeutic form of self-expression which they have stifled for too long because of fear and anxiety.

Or what about playing an instrument? Though a large

percentage of us learn the piano as children, few continue to play into adulthood. However, the ability to read music remains, and can be channelled into playing a recorder, an electronic keyboard (the simple ones are not expensive), or some other instrument you have never before had the time or opportunity to learn. As with singing, there will be classes, a local orchestra or jazz group, or an amateur society to join. Perhaps there is a children's dance group or adult keep-fit class in need of an accompanist.

If you love music but can neither sing nor play an instrument, you could help with organising performances, with publicity, selling tickets or counting the cash after the concert. This participation gives a feeling of involvement – you cannot be isolated if you are part of a group activity.

Painting and drawing This is perhaps one of the most exciting, undiscovered talents. Few people have really tried to draw or paint since art classes at school, and if they showed no particular flair at that time have never developed what skills they may have had. Yet statistics show that a surprising number of people who join painting or drawing classes later in life produce work of artistic merit which also expresses their feelings.

As a box of water colours costs very little, it might be a good idea to make your first attempt at painting in the privacy of your room. Most people have more ability than they realise – because they have never before given time to 'trying their hand'. Even small talents can open doors, give confidence and gain the admiration of others – all much needed when you are feeling lonely and insecure.

Reading Although this is a lone pastime, good writing evokes a response – you may laugh out loud or cry, be quite scared by a mystery story, or travel the world with an adventurer. If you are unable to see well or are tired and dispirited, you could try large print books which make reading so much easier and are colour categorised as romance (blue), mysteries (black), Westerns (orange), historical novels (purple), non-fiction (green) and general fiction (red).

Scrabble As you need a partner for scrabble, how do you find other players? You could mention your interest to neighbours who might know of another enthusiast in your area who would welcome the invitation to come and have a game; or there may be potential partners among the members of a local community organisation, luncheon club or day centre.

If you know a social worker, district nurse or another person who visits in the neighbourhood you could ask them to suggest some interested people. Of course, a bridge or whist drive also requires your getting a game together, but the effort involved in organising any of these games will yield many benefits.

Writing Everybody has a tale to tell, for each life is a reflection of the times. If you are in the over-50 age group, you will remember life during wartime, with ration books, the evacuation, and a host of incidents, both tragic and amusing, unknown to the young people of today. If only you could write down some of your memories. In most localities there is a writers' circle, where people who enjoy writing get together to compare notes, listen to each other's stories, perhaps you have guest speakers, and discuss markets where their work might be sold.

Do not make the mistake of worrying that everyone who attends a writers' workshop will be an expert, with published work to their credit. You will usually find that the majority attend just for the pleasure of putting thoughts down on paper.

In addition to classes or discussion groups, there are also local history societies where someone with a clear recollection of events, but no writing ability, could find a collaborator to help with the task of getting a personal account down on paper. The local library may also hold exhibitions about the area – how it has changed, which shops once existed, and you could add your personal memories of times gone by.

Directory of Useful Organisations

The organisations described in this chapter have been arranged according to the subjects listed below which are also covered in other chapters in the book. In all cases a stamped addressed envelope should accompany any inquiry for reply from an organisation.

Arts, crafts and pastimes
Bereavement
Carer's support
Dating and friendship agencies
Divorce and separation
Education
Grandparents' rights
Health care
Holidays
Penfriend contacts
Pensioners' support
Pet care
Sports and fitness
Voluntary organisations
Women's organisations

Arts, Crafts and Pastimes

Amateur Music Association
Encourages all forms of music and runs 'Get Back to Music' campaign.

c/o Music Department
City of Manchester
Education Committee
Medlock Junior School
Wadeson Road
Manchester M3 9UR

British Association of Barber-shop Singers
To encourage growth of barber-shop harmony singing.

19 Norwood Avenue
Alperton
Wembley HA0 1LX
Tel: 01-736 1212
ext 3490

British Red Cross Society
Trains people to provide community service skills, such as First Aid.

9 Grosvenor Crescent
London SW1X 7EJ
Tel: 01-253 5454

British Theatre Association
Drama training for amateurs and advisory service on all facets of theatre.

Darwin-Infill Building
Regents College
Inner Circle
Regents Park
London NW1 4NS
Tel: 01-935 2571

English Folksong and Dance Society
Encourages practice of song and dance

Cecil Sharp House
2 Regents Park Road
London NW1 7AX
Tel: 01-485 2206

National Association of Flower Arranging Societies of Great Britain
Has list of local groups and classes.

21a Denbigh Street
London SW1V 2HF
Tel: 01-828 5145

St John Ambulance
Provides training in life-saving, caring for sick and injured people.

1 Grosvenor Crescent
London SW1X 7EX
Tel: 01-235 5231

Scrabble Club Coordinator
Has list of local scrabble clubs.

42 Elthiron Road
London SW6 4BW
Tel: 01-731 2631

SESAME
*Makes possible a fuller life for handi-
capped people through dance and
movement.*

27 Blackfriars Road
London SE1 8NY
Tel: 01-633 9690

SHAPE
*Creates opportunities for mentally and
physically disabled and elderly people to
participate in arts activities.*

1 Thorpe Close
London W10 5LX
Tel: 01-960 9245

Bereavement

CRUSE
*Counselling, advice and opportunities
for social contacts to all widows and
widowers. Over 130 branches.*

126 Sheen Road
Richmond
Surrey TW9 1UR
Tel: 01-940 4818

Gay Bereavement Project
*Supportive advice in bereavement of a
partner of the same sex.*

Unitarian Rooms
Hoop Lane
London NW11 8BS
Tel: 01-837 7324

National Association for Widows
*Advice, literature and local branches, also
campaigns for widows' rights.*

Neville House
14 Waterloo Street
Birmingham B2 5UG
Tel: 021-643 8348

Carers' Support

(See also the organisations listed under Health Care)

Carers National Association
*Information and self-help encouragement
for carers of disabled or elderly people.*

21/23 New Road
Chatham
Kent ME4 4JQ
Tel: 0634 813981

Crossroads (Association of Cross-roads Care Attendant Schemes)
Provides trained home care for handicapped people.

HEAD OFFICE
94 Cotton Road
Rugby
Warwickshire CV21 3AQ
Tel: 0788 73653

NORTHERN IRELAND
87 University Street
Belfast BT7 1DL
Tel:0232 231105

SCOTLAND
24 George Square
Glasgow G2 1EG
Tel: 041-226 3793

Disabled Living Foundation
Extensive information on aids for disabled people.

384 Harrow Road
London W9 2HU
Tel:01-289 6111

Disability Alliance
Provides advice and publishes annual rights handbook.

25 Denmark Street
London WC2H 8NS
Tel: 01-240 0806

GLAD (Greater London Association for the Disabled)
For enquiries and leaflets.
Branches throughout London.

336 Brixton Road
London SW9 7AA
Tel: 01-274 0107

Dating and Friendship Agencies

Dateline
Write for free details about introductions

23 Abingdon Road
London W8 6AM
Tel: 01-938 1011

GEMMA (Lesbians with/without disabilities)
Aims to lessen isolation of lesbians and to publicise their needs.

BM, Box 5700
London WC1N 3XX

London Friend
For homosexuals.

BM Friend
London WC1N 3XX
Tel: 01-837 3337
7.30-10pm

WOMEN ONLY
Tel: 01-837 2782
Thursday 7.30-10pm

National Federation of 18 + groups
For network of local groups for people
aged 18-30.

Nicholson House
Old Court Road
Newent, Glos
Tel: 0531 821210

Old Friends
Introduction service for people over 40.

18a Highbury New Park
Highbury
London N5 2DB
Tel: 01-226 5432

Divorce and Separation

Gingerbread
Local groups for one-parent advice and
information.

33 Wellington Street
London WC2E 7BN
Tel: 01-240 0953

National Council for the Divorced
and Separated
Social activities and holiday scheme.
Counselling service in several regions
operates a postal advisory service.

13 High Street
Little Shelford
Cambridge CB2 5ES
Tel: 021-588 5157

National Federation of Solo Clubs
Over 700 clubs for divorced, widowed
or separated people.

Room 8, Ruskin
Chambers
191 Corporation Street
Birmingham B4 6RY
Tel: 021-236 2879

Education

National Extension College
Wide range of correspondence and home study courses.

18 Brooklands Avenue
Cambridge CB2 2HW
Tel: 0223 63465

Open University
Degree and short courses.

Enquiry Office
PO Box 71
Bucks MK7 6AA
Tel: 0908 653212

University of the Third Age (U3A)
Courses run locally on variety of topics. No qualifications required, none given.

6 Parkside Gardens
London SW19 3EY
Tel: 01-947 0401

Workers' Educational Association
Classes organised to meet local demands with special rates for pensioners. Also runs weekend courses and residential summer schools in the UK and abroad.

9 Upper Berkeley Street
London W1H 8BY
Tel: 01-402 5608/9

Grandparents' Rights

National Association of Grandparents
Campaigns for access to grandchildren.

8 Kirklee Drive
Ashington
Kent NE63 9RD

POPETS (Parents of Parents Eternal Triangle)
Counsels grandparents seeking access to grandchildren.

15 Calder Close
Higher Compton
Plymouth PL3 6NT
Tel: 0752 77036

Health Care

Alcoholics Anonymous
Autonomous local groups offer friendship and support for people with drink problems.

PO Box 1
Stonebow House
Stonebow
York YO1 2NJ
Tel: 0904 644026

Al-Anon Family Groups
*A worldwide fellowship providing
support for families of alcohol
victims.*

61 Great Dover Street
London SE1 4YF
Tel: 01-403 0888

Al-Ateen
*Offers support for teenagers affected by
an alcoholic relative.*

As above

Alcohol Concern
*Charity and resources centre for local
services and self-help groups.*

305 Gray's Inn Road
London WC1X 8QF
Tel: 01-833 3471

**Alternative and Orthodox Medicine
Clinic**
*Information about treatments and
therapies, also on cosmetic surgery.*

PO Box 598
Harley House
Marylebone Road
London NW1 5HW
Tel: 01-486 7490/8087

Alzheimer's Disease Society
Advice, literature and local groups.

Bank Buildings
Fulham Broadway
London SW6 1EP
Tel: 01-381 3177

Anorexic Aid
*Offers support and self-care advice for
sufferers from anorexia or bulimia
nervosa.*

The Priory Centre
11 Priory Road
High Wycombe
Bucks
Tel: 0494 21431

Arthritis Care
*Information and advice on benefits and
holidays for disabled people.*

6 Grosvenor Crescent
London SW1X 7ER
Tel: 01-235 0902

Back Pain Association
*Promotes exchanges between doctors
and osteopaths. For leaflets and local
groups send SAE.*

31-33 Park Road
Teddington
Middlesex TW11 0AB
Tel: 01-977 5474

British Deaf Association
*Information, local societies and services.
Also runs courses and holidays.*

38 Victoria Place
Carlisle
Cumbria CA1 1HU
Tel: 0228 48844

British Diabetic Association
Information, leaflets and national network of local groups.

10 Queen Anne Street
London W1M 0BD
Tel: 01-323 1531

British Epilepsy Association
Practical help, information and counselling.

Anstey House
40 Hanover Square
Leeds LS3 1BE
Tel: 0532 439393

British Migraine Association
Provides free introductory booklet for sufferers.

17a High Street
Byfleet, Surrey
Tel: 09323 52468

British Red Cross (Aids for the Disabled)

Address for local services listed in telephone directory or at community centres.

British Tinnitus Association
For sufferers from 'noises in the head'.

105 Gower Street
London WC1E 6AH
Tel: 01-387 4803

Chest, Heart and Stroke Association
Counselling, literature, local groups and volunteer visiting service.

Tavistock House North
Tavistock Square
London WC1H 9JE
Tel: 01-387 3012

Depressives Association
Local self-help groups support people suffering from depression.

PO Box 5
Castle Town
Portland
Dorset DT5 1BQ

Disabled Living Foundation
Information on all aspects of daily living for disabled persons. Contact for local incontinence advisers.

380-384 Harrow Road
London W9 2HU
Tel: 01-289 6111

Health Education Authority
Information on health, nutrition and exercise. Local units listed under health authority in telephone book.

Hamilton House
Mabledon Place
London WC1H 9TX

Tel: 01-631 0930

Kanga Advisory Service
  For information/advice on
  incontinence.

225 Bath Road
Slough
Berks SL1 4AU

MIND (National Association for
Mental Health)
  For local MIND groups, information
  and private therapy centres.
  Associations also in Scotland, Northern
  Ireland and Wales.

22 Harley Street
London W1N 2OE
Tel: 01-637 0741
Bookshop: 4th Floor
24-32 Stephenson Way
London NW1 2HD

Myalgic Encephalomyelitis
Association
  For self-help groups, information and
  referral to experienced doctors.

PO Box 8
Stanford-le-Hope
Essex SS17 8EX
Tel: 9375 642466
Mon-Thurs, Mornings only

National Osteoporosis Society
  Offers preventive and remedial advice
  on spinal degeneration.

Barton Meade House
PO Box 10
Radstock
Bath BA3 3YB
Tel: 0761 32472

National Society for Cancer Relief
  For contact with Macmillan Nursing
  Service.

Anchor House
15-19 Britten Street
London SW3 3TZ
Tel: 01-351 7811

Open Door Association
  Counsels agoraphobics.

447 Pensby Road
Heswall
Wirral L61 9PQ

Royal National Institute for
the Deaf
  Technical, social and library services;
  also displays environmental aids.

105 Gower Street
London WC1E 6AH
Tel: 01-387 8033

Phobic Action
  Develops self-help groups for sufferers
  of phobias and extreme anxiety.

547/551 High Road
Leytonstone
London E11 4PR
Tel: 01-558 3463

Society of Chiropodists
Information on all foot problems

53 Welbeck Street
London W1M 7HE
Tel: 01-486 3381/4

TRANX (UK) **Ltd**
*Advice and referral service to sufferers
of withdrawal symptoms from minor
tranquillisers.*

25a Masons Avenue
Wealdstone
Middlesex HA3 5AH
Tel: 01-427 2065

Holidays

**British Trust for Conservation
Volunteers**
Arranges volunteer holidays.

36 Mary's Street
Wallingford
Oxfordshire OX10 0EV
Tel: 0491 39766

**British University Accommodation
Consortium**
For information on university holidays.

Box 184
University Park
Nottingham NG7 2RD
Tel: 0602 504571

Countrywide Holidays Association
*Walking and other activity holidays
in Britain and abroad.*

Birch Heys
Cromwell Range
Manchester M14 6HU
Tel: 061-225 1000

Holiday Care Service
*Free information and advice on holiday
opportunities in UK and abroad for
elderly and disabled people.*

2 Old Bank Chambers
Station Road
Horley
Surrey RH6 9HW
Tel: 0293 774 535

Holiday Fellowship
*Walking and special interest holidays
in Britain and abroad.*

142 Great North Way
London NW4 1EG
Tel: 01-203 3381

**Major and Mrs Holt's Battlefield
Tours**
*Visits war areas, Flanders to Falklands,
staying at local hotels.*

15 Market Street
Sandwich
Kent CT13 9DA

SAGA Holidays Plc
Specialises in holidays for people over 60.

Bouverie House
Middleburgh Square
Kent CT20 1AZ
Tel: 0303 47000

SPLASH (Single Parents and Special Holidays)
For parents and children, in Britain and abroad.

19 North Street
Plymouth PL4 9AH
Tel: 07552 674067

Penfriend Contacts

Agony Aunt Barbara Boston
(Val Marriott)
Runs a free penfriend service for men and women.

c/o Press Association
News Features
85 Fleet Street
London EC4P 4BE

Amnesty International
Members write letters on behalf of human rights victims.

5 Roberts Place
off Bowling Green Lane
London EC1R 0EJ
Tel: 01-251 8371

British Christian PenPal Association
Send SAE for details.

157 Tuffley Lane
Gloucester GL4 0NZ

Canada Calling
For exchange of audio tapes with Canadian penpals.

c/o R Jones
2502 Garden Street
Victoria
British Columbia
Canada

Conversation by Correspondence Through Friends by Post
Send SAE for details.

6 Bolin Court
Macclesfield Road
Wilmslow
Cheshire SK9 2AP

Esperanto Centre
Promotes use of this international language.

140 Holland Park Avenue
London W11 4UF

International Friendship League
Offers penfriend contacts in the UK and abroad. Send information about yourself.

PO Box 117
Leicester LE3 6EE

FOR CONTACTS ABROAD
Saltash
Cornwall

S Nasman
For English speaking penfriends in Sweden – write for details.

S. 82500
Iggesund
Sweden

SAGA Magazine
Runs a penfriend/partnership section for SAGA members only.

Address on page 96

STYLOPAL
For Braille penfriends

c/o Civic Centre
Newcastle-upon-Tyne
NE1 8PA

Pensioners' Support

Age Concern England/Greater London/Northern Ireland/Scotland/Wales

Addresses on inside back cover

Help the Aged
Raises funds for day centres, minibuses, housing repair schemes. Comprehensive publications list.

St James's Walk
London EC1R 0BE
Tel: 01-253 0253

National Federation of Retirement Pensions Associations
Publish 'Pensioners' Voice'.

14 St Peter's Street
Blackburn BB2 2HD
Tel: 0254 52606

Pensioners Link
Groups in London for welfare rights advice and practical help.

19 Balfe Street
London N12 9EB
Tel: 01-278 5501

Standing Conference of Ethnic Minority Senior Citizens
Campaigns for improvement of services for ethnic minority groups.

5 Westminster Bridge Rd
London SE1 7XW
Tel: 01-928 8108/0095

Pet Care

Battersea Dogs Home
*Finds homes for stray dogs
(23,000 a year).*

4 Battersea Park Road
London SW8 4AA
Tel: 01-622 3626

Blue Cross Animals Hospital
*Provides care for animals whose owners
cannot afford a private vet. Also offers
home-finding service for stray animals.*

1 Hugh Street
London SW1V 1QQ
Tel: 01-834 4224

Cats Protection League
*Rehabilitates and finds homes for
lost and stray cats.*

17 Kings Road
Horsham
West Sussex RH13 5PP
Tel: 0403 65566

Cinnamon Trust
*Provides sanctuary for pets if owners
die.*

68 Carn Brea Lane
Pool
Redruth
Cornwall TR15 3DS
Tel: 0209 217080

Guide Dogs for the Blind Association
Trains dogs for blind people.

Alexandra House
9 Park Street
Windsor
Berkshire SL4 1JR

SCOTLAND
104 West Campbell Street
Glasgow G2 4TY
Tel: 041-248 6065

Hearing Dogs for the Deaf
Trains dogs for deaf people.

c/o Tony Blunt
Little Close
Lower Icknield Way
Lewknor, Oxfordshire
Tel: 0844 53898

National Canine Defence League
*Runs rescue centres for unwanted and
stray dogs.*

1-2 Pratt Mews
London NW1 0AD
Tel: 01-388 0137

People's Dispensary for Sick Animals

For free professional veterinary treatment for sick and injured animals for owners unable to pay. Pet care leaflet also available.

PDSA
South Street
Dorking
Surrey RH4 2LB
Tel: 0306 81691
Tel: 0306 81691

Royal Society for the Prevention of Cruelty to Animals

Relieves suffering and promotes kinder treatment generally.

Causeway
Horsham
West Sussex RH12 1HG
Tel: 0403 64181

SCOTLAND
19 Melville Street
Edinburgh EH3 7PL
Tel: 031-225 6418

Royal Society for the Protection of Birds

For information and addresses of local groups.

The Lodge
Sandy
Bedfordshire SG19 2BR
Tel: 0767 80551

Sports and Fitness

British Sports Association for the Disabled

Co-ordinates sport and recreation for disabled people.

Hayward House
Barnard Crescent
Aylesbury
Bucks HP21 9PP
Tel: 0296 27889

Extend

Trained volunteers visit people at home to help them learn to exercise.

Mrs Penny Copple SRN
3 The Boulevard
Sheringham
Norfolk Nr26 8DD
Tel: 0263 822479/842355

Fellowship of Cycling Old-timers

Provides friendship for cyclists over 50 and encourages local group activities.

2 Westwood Road
Marlow
Bucks SL2 2AT
Tel: 06284 3235

Iyenga Yoga Institute
Information on classes and qualified teachers.

223 Randolph Avenue
London W9 1NL
Tel: 01-624 3080

Keep Fit Association
Organises local exercise classes with trained tutors.

16 Upper Woburn Place
London WC1H 0QP
Tel: 01-387 4349

Ramblers' Association
Local groups arrange walks. Reduced membership for pensioners.

1-5 Wandsworth Road
London SW18 2LJ
Tel: 01-582 6878

Relaxation for Living
For details about relaxation classes tapes and leaflets and information about publications.

29 Burwood Park Road
Walton on Thames
Surrey KT12 5LH

Sports Council
Funds local initiatives including some arts and crafts courses. Write for local and regional facilities.

16 Upper Woburn Place
London WC1H 0QP
Tel: 01-388 1277
SCOTLAND
1 St Colme Street
Edinburgh EH1 3SA
Tel: 031-225 8411

Women's League of Health and Beauty
Supplies list of classes and booklets of exercises.

18 Charing Cross Road
London WC2H 0HR
Tel: 01-240 8456

Women's Organisations

A Woman's Place
Resource centre for women's information and local groups.

Hungerford House
Victoria Embankment
London WC2

Fawcett Library
Principal UK resource for women's history and studies.

City of London Poly
Old Castle Street
London E1 7NT
Tel: 01-283 1030

National Federation of Women's Institutes.
Crafts and cultural activities for country-based women.

39 Eccleston Street
London SW1 9NT
Tel: 01-730 7212

National Union of Townswomen's Guilds
Emphasises citizenship and offers leisure facilities.

75 Harborne Road
Edgbaston
Birmingham B15 3DA
Tel: 021-455 6868

National Women's Register
Nationwide groups for discussion and social activities.

c/o Antoinette Ferraro
245 Warwick Road
Solihull
West Midlands B92 7AH
Tel: 021-706 1101

Scottish Women's Rural Institute
Crafts and cultural activities.

42 Herlot Row
Edinburgh EH3 6ES

Women Welcome Women
International friendship network by correspondence and hospitality.

8a Chestnut Avenue
High Wycombe
Bucks HP11 1DJ
Tel: 0494 39481

Booklist

The publications listed below are grouped according to subjects discussed in the text. Some of the older books may only be available in the library. The more recent ones can be purchased in a bookshop. Those published by Age Concern England can be ordered by post on receipt of a cheque or postal order.

Health Care

Eating Well on a Budget, Age Concern England, 1987, £1.50

50 Plus Life Guide, Dr Miriam Stoppard, Dorling Kindersley, 1984

Know Your Medicines, Pat Blair, Age Concern England, 1985, £3.75

The Foot Care Book, Judith Kemp, Age Concern England, 1988, £2.95

The Magic of Movement, Laura Mitchell, Age Concern England, 1988, £3.95

Activities and Crafts

The Blandford Book of Traditional Handicrafts, John Rome, Blandford Press, 1981

Reader's Digest Manual of Handicrafts, 1982

Matchmaker (penfriend magazine, monthly), Chorley, Lancs.

Holidays

Holidays and Travel Abroad; A Guide for Disabled People, Royal Association for Disability and Rehabilitation, 1988

Housing

Housing Options for Older People, David Bookbinder, Age Concern England, 1987, £2.50

Sharing Your Home, Christine Orton, Age Concern England, 1988, £1.95

Using Your Home as Capital, Cecil Hinton, Age Concern England, £1.95

Owning Your Home in Retirement, National Housing and Town Planning Council, Age Concern England, 1987, £1.50

Mental Health

Anxiety; Self-Help for Your Nerves, Dr Claire Weeks, Angus & Robertson, 1986

Beginnings; A Book for Widows, B J Wylie, Allen & Unwin, 1986

Body Language, G Wainwright, Hodder & Stoughton, 1985

Depression, Dorothy Rowe, Routledge & Kegan Paul, 1983

Loneliness, Dr Tony Lake, Sheldon Press, 1980

Meeting People is Fun, Dr Phyllis M Shar, Sheldon Press, 1979

The Shy Person's Guide to Life, Michael Bentine, Grafton, 1985

Staying Together, Reginald Beech, John Wiley, 1985

Retirement

What Every Woman Should Know About Retirement, Edited by Helen Franks, Age Concern England, 1987, £4.50

Your Rights 1988/89; A Guide to Money Benefits for Retired People, Age Concern England, £1.50

Your Taxes & Savings 1988/89, Age Concern England, £2.50

Choice (magazine), *Yours* (newspaper), available from Choice Publications, Apex House, Oundle Rd. Peterborough PE2 9NP